T0228746

Russian Imperialism and the Medieval Past

PAST IMPERFECT

Further Information and Publications
www.arc-humanities.org/our-series/pi

Russian Imperialism and the Medieval Past

Ivan Foletti

British Library Cataloguing in Publication Data

A catalogue record for this book is available from the British Library.

© **2024, Arc Humanities Press, Leeds**

ISBN (print) 9781802701760
e-ISBN (PDF) 9781802702385
e-ISBN (EPUB) 9781802702392

www.arc-humanities.org

Printed and bound in the UK (by CPI Group [UK] Ltd), USA (by Bookmasters), and elsewhere using print-on-demand technology.

To Asja, Asu, Daria, Nastya, Rita, Pavel, Olga,
and all my other dear ones from Ukraine and Russia,
who were driven out of their homes by imperialism.

Contents

List of Illustrations

A Word by Way of Introduction

When I first visited Moscow in 2000, I saw a vibrant city bursting with life and incredible opportunities. It was a city where you could get married on the spot at three in the morning and then go to a sushi restaurant to celebrate (there were very few of them in Central and Western Europe then), or go to a rock club where books that had been banned for seventy years were sold and read. Even the university I visited then was a lively institution full of enthusiastic people. But, at the same time, Moscow was in many ways a wild and dangerous city. It was not advisable to cross the road if a car was in plain sight. Such situations could end in death, as happened to the husband of one of my acquaintances: he was hit by an official's black car in a pedestrian crossing. His widow lost the subsequent court case and Russia lost a poet. But it wasn't just about cars. Especially in the evening, the streets were not safe at all. Violent criminal activity was the norm in Moscow life. The wild 1990s were dawning, a time when the world of ordinary Russians literally collapsed after the fall of the Bolshevik regime and during the five hundred days of transition from socialism to capitalism. Some prominent members of the former regime, and some from organized crime, came to power. For everyone else, times were indeed hard. They faced runaway inflation, the disintegration of the welfare state, and violence on daily basis. Moscow was a city of contradictions. Despite all this, I must confess that for me it was an absolutely enchanting encounter (although, this was

Fig. 1: Vote for Putin—the only solution!, 2012. Photo courtesy of D. Kyndrová. Used with permission.

perhaps due to my age) that changed the course of my whole life. If it had not been for this trip, I might never have learned Russian, or begun to work on the history of Russian scholarship and imperialism, and, therefore, I would never have written the book you are now holding in your hands.

I returned to Moscow regularly. The more time I spent there, the more I realized the incredible cultural and human potential that lies there. The community of people I befriended were publishing books and working at the institution MEMORIAL (banned just before the military invasion of Ukraine began in 2022). These friends were also connected by their concern for people with mental disabilities, who had been, somehow, forgotten by the structures of the collapsed state. Helping the forgotten and needy, cerebral discussions, reading poetry, and a sense of a kind of unreal, wild freedom made the environment circling about this group one of hazy, intellectual attraction—I could not help but fall in love with it. Since my first visit, however, I have also begun to encounter far more poignant moments. Reminders of the past regime and the injustice of the current one were, and are, evident at every turn. Also visible are the creeping interconnection between various power structures, including the semi-mafia figures of the oligarchs with representatives of the church and the state apparatus. Since 1999, this interconnection has been led by an ambitious, once young man with a very problematic past, whose formation and experience he gained through the KGB. His name is Vladimir Putin [Fig. 1]. In this incredibly dangerous, and at the same time attractive chaos, a new order began to emerge, deeply rooted in, what is my opinion, the worst thing to characterize the country since the nineteenth century: the secret police.

* * *

In June 2020, the Church of the Resurrection of Christ, the main cathedral of the Armed Forces of the Russian Federation, was consecrated near Moscow. It was completed on May 9 of that year and became a tangible part of the celebrations of the seventy-fifth anniversary of the Soviet Union's victory over Nazi Germany [Figs. 2–3]. The ambitions of the building itself, however, were much greater, as they were a tribute to "the heroic deeds of the Russian people in all wars." During the construction of this 95-metre-high monumental cathedral, information was leaked to the media about the decoration of the interior with mosaics that were supposed to depict both Joseph Stalin as the victor of World War II and Vladimir Putin as the conqueror of Crimea in 2014. According to the official version presented by the Russian media, Putin's likeness was removed from the cathedral at his own request—a decision interpreted as a gesture of humility:

Fig. 2: Main Cathedral of the Russian Armed Forces,
Moscow Oblast, 2020. Photo courtesy of Sergey Sebelev.

Fig. 3: Ceremony of consecration of the Main Cathedral of the
Russian Armed Forces, Moscow Oblast, 2020. Photo courtesy
of Ministry of Defence of the Russian Federation.

Fig. 4: Mosaic
with Putin's image in the Main
Cathedral of the Russian Armed Forces.
Drawing by Janette Rendeková, 2024.
Used with permission.

Bishop Stefan of Klin explained to the RIA Novosti the situation with the mosaic depicting Vladimir Putin and other Russian politicians. According to him, the panel was made in a workshop, it has never been in the cathedral, and they decided not to display the part with the politicians. The decision to replace it was made by the artistic council, and it was based on the position of Putin himself. "By and large, this is the right approach, so we must agree with the opinion of the first person of the state," said Bishop Stephen [Fig. 4].[1]

However, when the president visited the cathedral for the first time in the early summer of that year, the reality was evident. In the first place, it was another step linking "throne and altar," a practice that can be observed with the Russian Federation since the 1990s. The president walked around the temple accompanied by the patriarch and the Minister of

---

1 "В РПЦ объяснили ситуацию с мозаикой с Путиным в храме Вооруженных сил [The Russian Orthodox Church Explained: The Situation with Putin's Mosaic in the Temple of the Armed Forces]," *Риа Новости* [Ria News], May 1, 2020; https://ria.ru/20200501/1570856062.html.

Fig. 5: Cathedral of Christ the Saviour, Moscow, beginning of the twentieth century.

Fig. 6: Postcard with the Church of Saviour on Blood, Saint Petersburg, 1910s.

Defence, kissing icons, bowing to sacred objects—and yet his body language clearly communicated that he was the master of this space. The military cathedral served to enshrine an idea that has become central to the Putin administration in recent years: that Putin himself is the rightful successor to the greatest heroic leaders of Russia and the USSR. In the more than twenty years since my first visit, the Russian Federation has changed so fundamentally that this rhetoric no longer surprised anyone. The national media enthusiastically reported on the event, while the international media ignored it or presented it without detailed comment.

The desire to depict the leaders of the Russian Empire, the USSR, and the Russian Federation was a key element in the conception of the entire temple. Therefore, it is still an open question as to why Putin's portrait was abandoned at the very end. However, this question is secondary, because even without his likeness the idea of the temple is unambiguous. The chosen concept and visual language of the whole building consciously articulates its subordination to the regime. At first glance, the exterior of the cathedral can be seen as a synthesis of two key Russian buildings from the nineteenth century. The first of these is Moscow's Christ the Saviour Cathedral, which was built as a solemn memorial to Russia's victory over Napoleon (1812): "meant to be a token of thanks to God for the salvation of the fatherland, and memorial to the fallen and, above all, the national monument, meant to commemorate the victory achieved by the join forces of the whole Russian Nation."[2] [Fig. 5] The second monument, which undeniably served as a model for the cathedral, partly bears the same consecration. This is the Cathedral of the Resurrection of Christ the Saviour on the Blood in Saint Petersburg,

---

2 K. Foletti, *The Cathedral of Christ the Saviour and Russia's Self-perception* (Master's thesis, Universität Wien, 2016), 7. On the Cathedral of Christ the Saviour in Moscow, see also E. Kirichenko, *Moscow's Cathedral of Christ the Saviour: Its Creation, Destruction, and Rebirth 1813-1997*, trans. T. H. Hoisington (Moscow: Smashwords Edition, 2012).

which was built at the turn of the nineteenth and twentieth centuries on the site where Tsar Alexander II was assassinated in 1881 (incidentally, the same tsar who freed the Russian serfs in 1861) [Fig. 6].

Dimitry Smirnov, the architect of the 2020 cathedral, thus, explicitly turned to the past and, in a language inherent to traditional neo-styles, wanted to show the unity or continuity between the past and the present. In the case of Smirnov's project, however, the demonstration of this continuity did not end only at the level of architecture: the overall composition and the incorporation of other artistic media is no less eloquent. Glass mosaic—which was also used in the case of the aforementioned Saint Petersburg Cathedral—was employed for its perceived artistic lineage in "Russian" heritage regions. This is an artistic technique traditionally associated with the period of Late Antiquity and with the monuments of the Eastern Roman Empire, so-called "Byzantium," where the tradition of this shimmering medium survived until the fourteenth century.[3] Thus, on a visual and conceptual level, Putin's Russia clearly draws not only on nineteenth-century tsarist representation, but also implicitly (and no less emphatically) on the tradition of the "medieval" and "Byzantine" world.

This was a logical choice for Putin, of course, because the art of the last Romanovs also referred to medieval prototypes. But why should the art of the twenty-first century refer to the art of Tsarist Russia, which made the Middle Ages the guarantor of its prestige? For those people who have consumed very distorted but popularized ideas about the

---

3 The notion of "Byzantium" is an ex-post construction used to define the Eastern Roman Empire only from the early modern period on, i.e., after this state disappeared with the fall of Constantinople in 1453. On this notion see I. Foletti and A. Palladino, "Byzantium as a Political Tool (1657–1952): Nations, Colonialism and Globalism," in *Byzantium in the Popular Imagination: The Modern Reception of the Byzantine Empire*, ed. M. Kulhánková and P. Marciniak (London: Bloomsbury, 2023), 45–66.

so-called "dark" Middle Ages, Putin's choice may appear to be an attempt to identify with the brutality of the pre-modern world. But the opposite is true: like Putin, the Romanovs (and not only them) used references to the past as tools to manipulate the perception of history. In other words, the connection to the past is used by current ruler(s) in an attempt to justify behaviour. But what behaviour is this intended to justify? Such a question seeks out the very essence of Russian statehood over the last centuries. The answer, of course, is located in the belief in an imperial right to rule. Byzantium plays a key role in this would-be right of succession, for it was one of the most powerful and longest-lasting empires of the past, and one that the Russian Empire has always longed to build upon. The image of the cathedral, built only three years ago, directly invites reflection on the relationship between art and imperialism, which we generally perceive as the conquering, expanding, and usually militant policy of a state.[4] It also opens the question of how the Russian Federation today uses (and abuses) the artistic representations of its predecessors: tsarist Russia and the USSR.

This book reflects on the role of art and the humanities (especially history and art history) within the power ambitions of given regimes or political parties. It primarily aims to reflect on the nature and representation of tsarist imperialism in the nineteenth century. Next, I will briefly present how a similar strategy, albeit in a seemingly completely opposite ideological vein, was employed by the Soviet Union. Finally, I will briefly reflect on the abuse of the past in contemporary Russia since the fall of the Soviet Union. The subject of Russian imperialism is one of the themes that has occupied me throughout my life, and this book is one of the results of many years of research. It will, therefore, have all the parameters of

---

4 For a definition of the concept of imperialism see, e.g., that of the *Oxford Learner's Dictionary*: 1. a system in which one country controls other countries, often after defeating them in a war; 2. the fact of a powerful country increasing its influence over other countries through business, culture, etc.

a scholarly text, but at the same time it will be very personal. Although scholarship should try to interpret reality as objectively as possible, the subject—the scholar himself—is part of that reality, and his personality and commitment cannot be separated from the research. This is also why it seems fair to add that my aim is not simply to present the reader with the story of Russian imperialism and its representation, for I would also like to show how complicated the Russian political situation was (and remains). Imperialism expresses a state ideology that is often far removed from the lives of the people of the country it is supposed to represent. I would like this second voice, the voice of the people, which is certainly less vocal but no less important, to be heard within the book.

I would like to thank all those who made the publication of this book possible. First and foremost, my thanks go to Karolina Foletti, whose critical comments and original research were essential to this book. I am also very grateful to Margarita Khakhanova for her help with the conception of the illustration material and for her many consultations. Special thanks deserve my students Jana Černocká, Paulína Horvátová, Kateřina Jůzlová, and Zuzana Urbanová for their constant help. Without them this book could not have been written. I would also like to express my gratitude to Adrien Palladino and Kris Racaniello. For a person with an imperfect command of English, their work is invaluable. This book in its current form could not have been produced without the generous provision of images by Dana Kyndrová. Ms. Kyndrová has been photographing Russia for forty years and her photographs can explain this harrowing recent history far more efficiently than a long text.

Last but not least, I would like to thank Jana Černocká and Mark Černocký and their charitable company Energeia. They are the (electric) driving force that made the publication of this book possible.

I would like to dedicate this volume to the memory of Hans Belting. Hans was an incredible friend, and a constant source of inspiration. This book is also the result of our long discussions.

Chapter 1

The Russian Empire and Byzantium
From Napoleon to Nicholas II

Fig. 7: Demolition of the Alexander Nevsky Cathedral, Warsaw, 1924–1926.

Apparently, it happened without emotion: the workers came and slowly began to demolish. The work went on for two whole years (1924–1926) and, in the end, not one stone was left of the Alexander Nevsky Cathedral in Warsaw [Fig. 7] At the beginning of the twentieth century, Poland was a bastion of Catholicism, so the destruction of a church in the capital city may have seemed out of step with popular sentiment, but to destroy a church that had only been completed twelve years earlier at that time smacked of sensationalism. The emotions behind such a decision must have been very strong. As a precaution against inciting an impassioned response, the demolition took a civil form, that is, it was a systematic and respectful demolition. This was certainly intended to calm the sensitive atmosphere in which this sacrilegious action took place, but it did nothing to diminish the power of the gesture. Such a gesture can only be understood in the context of violent nineteenth-century Russian imperialism, which turned art and saints into instruments of propaganda and identity. The destruction of the temple was, indeed, one way to oppose Russia's expansionist policies.

Dreaming Byzantium

The story of Russian imperialism has deep historical roots. Its origins can be traced back to the time when Ivan IV, known as the Terrible (1547–1584) was crowned "Tsar of All Russia" in 1547. Although the tendency of rulers to expand their territories was the practice of all major European powers in the sixteenth century (think, for example, of the brutal colonial policies of the kingdoms of Spain and Portugal), a glance at the history of the Russian Empire reveals that expansionist endeavours characterized Russian statehood from the reign of Ivan IV onwards. However, every imperial power requires rhetorical weapons to defend its ambitions—or to speak bluntly, it needs "excuses" for the inevitable imperial atrocities. This has often been done through the smoke screen of defending religious issues, protecting the oppressed or, and this is crucial for our reflection, through historical law, i.e. in the defence of policies in the light of (real or entirely imagined) historical claims. Russian power made abundant use of these tools, and at least since the early nineteenth century it can be said that "historical law" gained more and more space and power, especially in the context of an increasingly clearly declared relationship with the Byzantine Empire.[1]

---

[1] Rakitin, "Byzantine Echoes in the Nineteenth Century Press." Where a short-form citation is provided, please consult the Further Reading at the end.

Fig. 8: Carl Leberecht and Johann Balthasar Gass, medal on the occasion of the birth of Grand Duke Konstantin Pavlovich, 1779. Photo courtesy of Fritz Rudolf Künker GmbH & Co. KG, Osnabrück, Lübke & Wiedemann KG, Leonberg. Used with permission.

Byzantium, one of the most powerful medieval and Christian empires, was repeatedly presented in Russian history as the source of the empire's imperial legitimacy. Ivan IV himself received his imperial title from the patriarch of Constantinople, who was to some extent seen as the guarantor of the continuity of the Eastern Empire even after the fall of Constantinople in 1453. Even Catherine II the Great (1762–1796), several centuries later, promoted a power rhetoric that directly related to the empire on the Bosporus.[2] Catherine was a monarch with an otherwise Enlightenment reputation, but during her reign the so-called "Greek Dream" was orchestrated, based on a utopian desire to "liberate" (from the Russian perspective) Constantinople from the hands of the Turks and to return it to the "bosom" of Christianity. This dream was justified by both historical and religious "arguments."[3] Although utopian, this "dream" also had a very concrete geo-political purpose.

2 H. C. d'Encausse, "Le rêve grec de Catherine II," in *La Méditerranée d'une rive à l'autre: culture classique et cultures périphériques*, ed. A. Laronde and J. Leclant (Paris: Académie des Inscriptions et Belles-Lettres, 2007), 1–8.

3 M. Heller, *Histoire de la Russie et de son Empire* (Paris: Perrin, 1997), 582–83.

It was to give Russia an outlet to the Mediterranean; if successful, it would have been a momentous change in the state of the tsars, who would have had access to one of the most important markets in Eurasia. It also produced a very concrete visual response, providing critical data for this volume, in the form of a medal designed by Carl Leberecht and Johann Balthasar Gass to mark the birth of Grand Duke Konstantin Pavlovich (1779–1831), grandson of Catherine. The reverse of this object depicts a silhouette of the Hagia Sophia [Fig. 8] A closer look at the medal, however, reveals an even more interesting detail: the Christian symbol par excellence, the cross, is depicted on the top of the dome and on the minarets. Russian ambitions were explicitly visualized: Catherine wanted to conquer Constantinople and continue the Byzantine tradition, a desire justified by Christian expansionism. It is interesting to note how, at the end of the eighteenth century, the idea of reconverting the building founded by Justinian I (527–565) back into a church was mobilized as an explicit symbol and implicit justification for the reconquest of the whole city. In this sense the current socio-political situation in Turkey is also not surprising, with the regime of president Erdoğan converting the Hagia Sophia museum—established by Mustafa Kemal Atatürk in 1935—into a mosque in 2020: whether one approves of it or not, Hagia Sophia remains a contentious symbol of power linking religion and politics on the Bosporus.

Interestingly, during Catherine's reign outward association with Byzantine heritage was probably limited to the imperial court, or perhaps even more restricted to the inner circle of the monarch herself as part of her powerful self-representation. Evidence of this can be gleaned from the rejection of such heritage associations by the vast majority of Russian elites even at the beginning of the nineteenth century. They followed the Enlightenment tradition begun under Peter the Great (1682–1721) and were still oriented towards a glorification of "Western" culture and, thus, were primed to disassociate from Byzantine heritage.

In early modern times, therefore, the idea of Byzantium as a mythical ancestor of Russia was present among elites—

even if some of them distanced themselves from this perceived lineage. Moreover, pragmatic, economic, and political reasons made Russian rulers dream of conquering Constantinople. However, these were distant dreams with the country facing, at least as far as the aristocracy was concerned, decidedly westward.

Russia, Napoleon, and Byzantium

The moment of rupture certainly comes with the Napoleonic Wars, which represented a particularly traumatic moment for Russia's traditionally Francophile elites. Indeed, the attack by the French emperor's troops, which led to the capture (and burning) of Moscow, prompted Russian intellectuals to question the country's role on the international chessboard. It is within this context that a significant change can be observed. Russian elites suddenly felt betrayed by the "West," and by France, in particular. This opened the previously closed debate on Russia's "directionality": should it orient itself towards the West, or towards the East? Some intellectuals, such as Pyotr Chaadayev (1794–1856), rejected the idea of "Byzantium" as the cradle of Russian culture. For others, however, it became the "promised land" on which Russian identity was to be built in the future. This historical identification of Russia with Byzantium was also supported by the Orthodox religion, which was installed in Kievan Rus' from Constantinople.

With the accession of the new Tsar Nicholas I (1825–1855) to the throne, disillusionment with the idealized West began to be reflected, and crucially for this book, in the visual representation of the empire. After years in which official Russian architecture mimicked that of the West, the tsar's entourage began to reflect on what image the Russian Empire should now have in the world. Looking at the design of the Cathedral of Christ the Saviour in Moscow, a building that accompanies us throughout this book, the reversal in the Russian Empire's attitude and orientation is obvious This building was originally designed by the architect Alexander Vitberg

Храмъ Христа Спасителя
проэктированный А. Л. Витбергомъ, на Воробьевыхъ горахъ, въ Москвѣ, но не осуществленный.

Fig. 9: Alexander Vitberg, project of the Cathedral of Christ Saviour, 1825. Photo from E. Tichomirov, *Храм Христа Спасителя в Москве (сооруженного по проекту А. Л. Витберга)* [Cathedral of Christ the Saviour in Moscow (Designed by A.L. Witberg)], Moscow, 1882.

Fig. 10: Jean-Baptiste Hilair, The Pantheon, 1795.

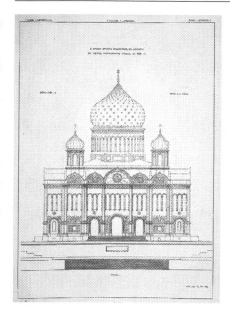

Fig. 11: Konstantin Thon, Project of the Cathedral of Christ the Saviour, 1838. Photo from G. Baranovsky, *Архитектурная Энциклопедия второй половины XIX века: Том I. Архитектура Исповеданий* [Encyclopedia of Architecture of the Second Half of the 19th Century: Vol. I, Religious Architecture], Saint Petersburg, 1902.

(1787–1855) in 1817, shortly after the defeat of Napoleon, and was intended to be a celebration of victory in the neoclassical style [Fig. 9]. Its appearance in his plans was ironically reminiscent of the Pantheon in Paris [Fig. 10]. For Nicholas I, however, the appearance of a building inspired by French neoclassicism, a style peculiar to the defeated enemy, became unacceptable. He commissioned the architect Konstantin Thon (1794–1881) to conceptualize a "truly new" and "Byzantine" design [Fig. 11]. The result was a building whose construction stretched into the 1860s. According to Thon, it was intended to relate to both to the greatest building of Eastern Christianity, Hagia Sophia in Constantinople, and to Russia's medieval past [Fig. 12].[4]

---

4 Thon, *Проекты церквей, сочиненные архитектором его императорского величества* [Church Designs Devised by the Imperial Architect].

Fig. 12: Hagia Sofia, Constantinople, 532–537.
Photo courtesy of the Library of Congress.

Fig. 13: Church of Archangel Michael, Moscow, 1505.

However, much more than Constantinople, the Moscow Cathedral of Christ the Saviour refers to Russian medieval and Renaissance monuments, such as the Cathedral of Arch-angel Michael in the Moscow Kremlin [Fig. 13]. This strange connection, neo-Byzantine in theory but neo-Russian in practice, is far from surprising: it shows how much the terms "medieval Russian" and "Byzantine" overlapped in nine-teenth-century thought. The choice of this visual style, which was to become the official national style of Russia by tsarist decree, was intended to refer to the imperial and medieval Byzantine roots of the Russian Empire, while at the same time legitimizing Russia's territorial ambitions.[5] Nicholas I, however, did not limit himself to defining a new style. Follow-ing the reflections of the then Minister of Education Sergey Uvarov (1786–1855), he decided that the new state doctrine of the empire would stand on three pillars, namely ortho-doxy, autocracy, and nation. The connection of these three concepts with the Byzantine tradition was logical. Not only did the tsarist title arrive in Russia from Constantinople, but Russian Orthodoxy was directly based on the Byzantine "pro-totype." The Orthodox Byzantine-Russian tradition based on autocracy was not only to become one of the building blocks of state identity, but gradually began to be used more and more clearly as a political argument to justify the territorial expansion of the empire.

The Russian Empire used a similar strategy as early as 1801, when it annexed the Kingdom of Kartli-Kakheti, a ter-ritory roughly equivalent to present-day Georgia. Russian imperial propaganda presented the political annexation of this ancient Caucasian culture as the logical consequence of a common Orthodox identity. In the words of the *Manifesto*, which was written between the reigns of Paul I (1796–1801) and Alexander I (1801–1825), it was the political consumma-tion of what was already a reality on the theological level, i.e.,

---

5 "Статья 218 Устава Строительного [Article 218 of the Statutes of the Construction]," 12.

Fig. 14: Caricature about the Russo-Turkish War, nineteenth century.

it was to unite two fraternal peoples long united by Orthodoxy into one.[6] In the years that followed, Georgia was alternately presented as a country united with Russia through its Orthodox identity and as an ancient part of the Byzantine Empire. It should have logically followed that Russia, as the heir of Byzantium, had succession rights over Georgia itself.

During the nineteenth century, Orthodoxy and its declared continuity with the Byzantine Empire became one of the arguments used to defend the tsar's often aggressive imperial policy. The Byzantine past was deployed by Russian propaganda to justify the gradual occupation of the entire Caucasus or military interventions in the Balkans, where the Russian Empire was (officially) supposed to protect the "Orthodox brothers" against the "Ottoman infidels." Wars with the Ottoman Empire were also justified by the Byzantine and Orthodox past: as in the case of Catherine the Great, these wars officially stemmed from desire to conquer Constantinople and reclaim it for the Orthodox world [Fig. 14].

---

6 "Манифест к грузинскому народу [Manifesto to the Georgian Nation]", 782–87.

In reality, however, it was about one of the obsessions of Russian foreign policy, namely access to the Mediterranean. The dream of the Russian tsars to sit on the imperial throne in Constantinople became one of the great themes of Russian expansionist efforts in the second half of the nineteenth century. For example, Alexander II (1855–1881) tried to conquer the city during the Russo-Turkish War (1877–1878) but was stopped by his Western Allies. Nicholas II (1896–1917) entered World War I with a similar desire in mind.

In a broader context, it seems important to recall that Nicholas I's choice to promote the neo-Byzantine style as the official style of the empire actually demonstrated—despite the rhetoric—that Russian elites belonged to a pan-European space. Indeed, the choice of medieval neo-historical styles to represent the identity of various (nascent or existing) states was one of the European constants during the nineteenth century. Despite its Slavophile position, Russia was an integral part of this discourse that united the entire continent.

Scholarship at the Service of the Empire

However, Russian imperial rhetoric and Byzantine identity were not only based on political ambitions. From the mid-nineteenth century onwards, Byzantine imperial and cultural "origins" were also supported by scholarly argumentation.[7] The first scholars working on medieval art, often still erudite amateurs, began to point out the undeniable continuity between the Eastern Roman Empire and that of Russia through the study of art and architecture. They considered, through these studies, that they could empirically demonstrate Russia's Byzantine roots. Ivan Sakharov (1807–1863) and Dimitry Rovinsky (1824–1895)—the former trained as a physician and the latter as a jurist—promoted the view that the entire history of Russian painting was derived from

---

7 M. Lidova, "The Rise of Byzantine Art and Archaeology in Late Imperial Russia," 120–60.

forty ancient Byzantine icons, all of which have survived in Russia. Although it was later revealed that these scholars actually had no idea what authentic medieval artistic production in the East Roman Empire actually looked like, their theses nevertheless provided a basis for demonstrating this desired continuity. Even Alexander Pushkin's peer and friend Grigory Gagarin (1810–1893), a Russian military officer and high-ranking civil servant who had studied architecture, attempted to formulate something of a "general" history of Christian architecture and decoration along these lines. Based on the similarities of visual and architectural elements in the conception and execution of the buildings he selected, he created a rather bold developmental series of connections and used it to link late antique Ravenna and Constantinople with nineteenth-century Moscow. Georgia played a key role in this story, as it was in the Caucasus that Gagarin believed the link between the Mediterranean and the Russian Empire was forged. Gagarin was also the first to question the aesthetics that were to be proper to the Russian Orthodox world. In his view, in fact, the "Western" style of landscape or portrait painting popular among the country's elites did not correspond to true Russian identity. The latter could be represented in his view only by a return to "Byzantine" and medieval models. In the middle of the century, he proposed an overhaul of the aesthetic paradigm at the academy of fine arts, but his proposal was strongly rejected. This was one of the first attempts to make neo-medieval style one of the constituent elements of private Russian culture.[8]

Gagarin was a "visionary" not fully understood by his contemporary artists and academics, but the situation would change rapidly in the following decades. Over the second half of the century, the importance (and necessity) of using a neo-Russian (or neo-Byzantine) style impressed itself among architects. Perhaps the most interesting figure in this regard

---

8 Gagarin, *Краткая хронологическая таблица в пособие истории византийского искусства* [A Short Chronological Table in the Handbook on the History of Byzantine Art].

was Nikolay Sultanov (1850–1908), who was convinced that the use of neo-Russian architectural repertoire was Russia's answer to the West and should be supported precisely for this reason.[9]

In the same years as Sultanov's activities, the importance of the medieval past in building the present touched increasingly broad sections of society, including amongst the first professional art historians. Foremost among them was Nikodim Kondakov (1844–1925), the founder of modern art history in Russia, who used his pen to provide arguments for the political ambitions of the Russian Empire.[10] It is enough to recall his studies on the South Caucasus, where he argued that the medieval art of this region, i.e. the art of Georgia and Armenia, was always the art of a province of the Byzantine Empire. The scholar also insisted that the art of these two regions were so similar that they could only be seen as the unique expression of a Byzantine provincialism. Today it is clear that this view, especially when it comes to architecture, does not hold water and is only taken up as a political position. The production of both these medieval states was always in dialogue with Byzantium, but at the same time they were quite clearly distinct and their relationship with that power was minimal in some periods.[11] Even Kondakov must have been at least partly aware of this, yet he acted in the interests of the Russian Empire. It is not surprising, therefore,

---

9 Sultanov, "Русское зодчество в западной оценке [Russian Architecture in Western Evaluation]".

10 L. Khrushkova, "Nikodim Pavlovich Kondakov," in *Personenlexikon zur Christlichen Archäologie*, vol. 2, ed. S. Heid and M. Dennert (Regensburg: Schnell and Steiner, 2012), 751–54; Foletti, *From Byzantium to Holy Russia*.

11 For a general reflection on the history of the region and some key monuments, see I. Foletti et al., *The Othering Gaze: Imperialism, Colonialism, and Orientalism*, in *Studies on Medieval Art in the Southern Caucasus (1801–1991)* (Brno: Viella 2023); M. Bacci et al., *Approaches to Sacred Space(s) in Medieval Subcaucasian Cultures* (Brno: Viella 2023).

that these theses were fabricated and resonated in the very years when Russia was trying to unite the cultures of Georgia and Armenia into one "province," the South Caucasus Governorate.[12] If the region could be reframed as a once provincial part of Russia's ancestral imperial power (Byzantium), then the regions could be seen as "naturally" connected to and, thus, rightfully subjugated by Russia.

Kondakov's involvement in the issue of Macedonia was even more evident, as the scholar used historical, artistic, and folkloristic arguments to argue that this country should be annexed to Bulgaria. For this endeavour, the scholar had even assembled a group made up of historians, philologists, and folklorists to evaluate the situation from all possible disciplinary angles. In writing the final publication, however, he was the sole author, as if he wanted to control the final product all the way through. In this case, too, Kondakov was probably deliberately deceiving. He knew very well that Macedonia was a multicultural state at that time, where at least three languages were spoken, and it was not (or should not have been) possible to assign it to one of the local nation-states only on the basis of cultural and historical arguments. Needless to say, he came to this conclusion, and such conclusions were fully consistent with Russian ambitions in the region.

Whatever Kondakov's inner motivation, I am convinced that he must have been aware to some extent that he was reshaping history. The question is how much he himself believed the stories he wove. What is certain, however, is that his scientific arguments clearly supported Russian political interests in the Balkans. Today, it is easy to condemn Kondakov in this respect because the extent of his manipulation of the past is now blatant. It is important to note, that there is no direct evidence for how aware he was of his transgressions. Even today, it is often difficult to admit or assess how much our opinions or research questions are able to approach

---

12 D. Gutmeyr, *Borderlands Orientalism or How the Savage Lost his Nobility: The Russian Perception of the Caucasus between 1817 and 1878* (Vienna: LIT, 2017).

objectivity or how much they are influenced by the times in which we live. After all, this book is also being written at a time when Russian imperialism is a very topical subject to consider. Even though I have been entwined with and working on this subject from the outset of my dissertation work in 2004, I am nevertheless (or precisely because of this) aware of the difficulty of determining where objectivity ends and subjectivity begins in research, and especially of how it is framed in scholarly or scientific outputs.[13]

Building the New Byzantium

In addition to propaganda, which involved scholars and intellectuals, the idea of Russian imperialism was also projected, as mentioned above, into the visual culture and architecture of the various newly acquired "provinces." It was art in the service of power that made the arguments of the tsarist milieu visible. In this sense, it seems important to remember that architecture and monumental art in general were the real mass media of those years. More or less elitist concepts filtered into public knowledge, precisely by the graces of monumental constructions.

This was particularly visible in Tbilisi, for example, where the construction of the Cathedral of Alexander Nevsky began in 1871 to celebrate the "subjugation" of the entire South Caucasus.[14] [Fig. 15] Nevsky, the thirteenth-century prince from Novgorod canonized by the Orthodox Church in the sixteenth century, was, and still is, a fundamental symbol of Russian statehood.[15] While the choice of consecration is unsurprising, the choice of the church's style was inter-

---

13 On this topic in general see e.g., R. J. Evans, *In Defence of History* (London: Granta, 1997).

14 Wortman, "The 'Russian Style' in Church Architecture," 101–229; R. Wortman, *Scenarios of Power*, 251.

15 A. Navrotskaya, "Aleksandr Nevskii: Hagiography and National Biography," *Cahiers du monde russe* 46, no. 1–2 (2005): 297–304.

Fig. 15: Cathedral of Alexander Nevsky, Tiflis (Tbilisi), 1890.

Fig. 16: The Church of Theotokos Kyriotissa, now Kalenderhane Mosque, Konstantinopol, twelfth century.
Photo courtsey of Stilbes.

esting for its surprising depth of observation and stylistic verisimilitude, as elaborated below. Indeed, architecturally, it represents the purest form of neo-Byzantine architecture imaginable. The architectural elements used on this building refer to several models from the periods of the greatest flowering of Byzantine architecture. The monumental dome of the building was reminiscent of Hagia Sophia in Constantinople from the sixth century: while the stereometric construction of the dome resting on four semi-domes was inspired by the latter, the style of the dome itself is actually based on later monuments in its continuous blind arcade. Large windows with *transennae*, in turn, match to later models such as the eighth-century church of Hagia Eirene in Constantinople. The shape of the windows and the blind arcade of the dome are reminiscent of those used within the first two centuries after 1000, such as the Church of Theotokos Kyriotissa (now Kalenderhane Mosque) in Istanbul, built in the first quarter of the eleventh century [Fig. 16]. Finally, striped masonry is a traditional phenomenon which was important in Constantinople but also throughout the Byzantine territory, the Balkans etc. until the fifteenth century. Thus, we can speak about a monument referring in various ways to the Byzantine past.

However, if we compare the temple in Tbilisi with the Cathedral of Christ the Saviour in Moscow, we notice a fundamental difference. In the case of Konstantin Thon's project (in reality inspired by Russian medieval and early modern architecture), the inspiration was conceptual, based on an idealized vision of what Byzantine architecture should have looked like, but without a real knowledge of medieval Byzantine buildings. The reference was largely rhetorical and not based on the imitation of concrete formal elements and shapes. In the case of the Tbilisi cathedral, on the contrary, we are confronted with a clear visual reference to medieval architecture. This can be explained within the context of a much deeper knowledge of the art of the empire of Constantinople in the last quarter of the nineteenth century, but also considering the popularity of neo-byzantine architecture in

Fig. 17: Cathedral of Alexander Nevsky, Sofia, 1882–1912.
Photo courtesy of M. Khakhanova, 2023. Used with permission.

Europe. The general framework of thought, however, remains unchanged at first sight. The architectural models of the past were used to justify the political ambitions of the empire in the present. Neo-Byzantine architecture, thus, acted as a visualization of Russian expansionism. In this thought, as the Caucasus belonged to the Byzantine Empire, it must belong to the Russian Empire. This colonial idea is made even more explicit when we consider the location of the building, which would be destroyed in the Stalin years: built atop the city of Tbilisi, then the capital of the Caucasus Viceroyalty, it ostensibly dominated the cityscape. Obviously, this domination was to extend, in the imaginations of its designers, to the entire region.

From this point of view, the cathedral with the same dedication to Nevsky and the same general structure, built in 1882 in Sofia, Bulgaria, is likewise interesting [Fig. 17]. The structural typology of the building—i.e., the "Hagia Sophia" type, the plan, the vault organization—clearly reminds Tbilisi, while further elements are referring directly to Russia: this is the case of the façade tower reminiscent of the Saint Petersburg Church of the Saviour and indeed a very common "Russian" element. Although Bulgaria was not directly part of the last Romanov Empire, it was under its protection throughout the second half of the nineteenth century. The official reason for the construction of the cathedral was to show gratitude to the Russian people for the liberation of the Bulgarians from Ottoman rule. In this case, then, the neo-Byzantine architecture associated with Alexander Nevsky as the Russian national saint was tangible proof that Bulgaria fell within the Russian sphere of influence.

The cathedral of the same dedication built in 1877 in Belgrade, Serbia, in memory of the Russian volunteers who died in the war with the Ottoman Empire, can be seen in a similar light. The original form of the cathedral is unknown, but the present structure, begun in 1912, has the parameters of the other neo-Byzantine buildings already mentioned. Thus, the architectural design, Neo-Byzantine artistic style, and dedication have become features that clearly indicate the influence of the Tsarist Empire. Exercise of power within the colonial phenomenon passes not only through a violent takeover of the annexed state, but through the silent contrition of allies. Bulgaria and Serbia were, to all intents and purposes, independent states. However, they needed to be part of the Russian orbit to secure a place on the European playing field. Accepting a Russian colonial visual language was, thus, a way for these states to define their strategic political positions. It is in this sense useful to recall how close the strategy adopted by the Russian Empire is to that of the Commonwealth—the great rival of the tsar empire throughout the nineteenth century—and its "soft power."

The dedication to Alexander Nevsky brings us back to the Warsaw cathedral mentioned at the beginning of this chapter. It was built in 1894–1912, officially for the needs of the local Orthodox community. It is well known that the Kingdom of Poland, officially called the Congress Poland from 1815 to 1915, was a very dissatisfied part of the Russian Empire at this time [Fig. 18]. After the uprising against Nicholas I in 1830–1831, which was cruelly suppressed, the kingdom lost most of its privileges. Over ten thousand Poles emigrated to

Fig. 18: Cathedral of Alexander Nevsky, Warsaw, 1894–1912.
Photo courtsey of the Library of Congress.

the West, and about eighty thousand were sent in chains to Siberia. This did not stop the Polish desire for independence; on the contrary, it rallied resistance. In January 1863, a second, larger uprising took place with even more dire consequences, leading to the complete end of Polish autonomy and a policy of forced Russification. According to some scholars, it was the 1863 uprising that showed the Russian Empire how

Fig. 19: Church of Saviour on Nereditsa, Novgorod, 1199. Photo courtesy of N. Rakitina, 2016. Used with permission.

dangerous nationalism could be to its existence.[16] Violent Russification can be seen from the Russian imperial perspective as a "logical" reaction to the manifestations of nationalism. In general, it shows the extent to which imperialism and nationalism, concepts typical of the nineteenth century, co-create each other.

In this context, the construction and the chosen style of the cathedral were an even more imperialist and political project. This time, it was not built in the neo-Byzantine style, but directly in the neo-Russian style. In its visuality, the church refers to Russian medieval models, such as the churches in Vladimir or Novgorod, which feature the now typical onion dome [Fig. 19]. The interior decoration—paintings and mosaics—was commissioned by Viktor Vasnetsov (1848–1926), a prominent painter of late-tsarist Russia. The presence of

---

16 See e.g., S. Kieniewicz, A. Zahorski, and W. Zajewski, *Trzy powstania narodowe: kościuszkowskie, listopadowe i styczniowe* [Three National Uprisings of Kościuszko: November and January] (Warsaw: Książka i Wiedza, 1994).

these two techniques, and mosaics particularly, implicitly refer not only to Russian culture but especially appeal to Byzantine imperial authority.

As explicitly stated in 1893 by Joseph Gurko (1828–1901), Russian general and governor of Poland in 1883–1894, the Warsaw cathedral, the tallest in the whole city, was to become a manifesto for the Russification of the whole country.[17] Dominating the skyline, the cathedral comprehensibly demonstrated Russian hegemony in Warsaw and proclaimed that Poland belonged politically and historically to Russia, at least according with its imperial rhetoric. It is not surprising, then, that this building was perceived by Poles as the embodiment of enormous moral and symbolic oppression. Thus, it was razed to the ground after the heated debate that followed the declaration of Polish independence.[18]

At the beginning of this chapter we asked how it was possible for the predominantly Catholic Poland to raze a church in the early twentieth century, and now we have an answer: to destroy this church was to destroy a symbol of Russian imperial occupation. The building and its demolition clearly testify to its importance for both Russian imperial and Polish national identity.

Conclusion

Neo-Byzantine and neo-Russian architecture, with its dedication to Alexander Nevsky, became in the second half of the nineteenth century the materialization and visualization of Russian imperial ambitions, and a tool to define the imperial sphere of influence. The shared history of two powerful empires became an argument for vast and aggressive geopolitics. Additionally, all great imperial empires, such as Great

---

17 Wortman, *Scenarios of Power*, 254–55.

18 A. Mironowicz, "The Destruction and Transfer of Orthodox Church Property in Poland, 1919–1939," *Polish Political Science Yearbook* 43 (2014): 405–20.

Britain and France, manifested themselves in a similar way at the end of the nineteenth century, albeit using divergent visual tools and strategies. In this respect, Russia at the end of tsarist rule followed (and co-created) the trend of world powers adopting imperialism and colonialism as standards of political strategy. Scholarship, science, and art became key tools in propaganda to justify territorial claims and interests. Of course, it was not only the historical sciences that entered the service of colonialism and imperialism, but also racial theories originating in the fields of biology and medicine, for example, were warmly supported by the rulers.

On a more general level, another aspect should be mentioned: this was (and in many respects still is) a world where the past was rebuilt (and re-invented) thanks to a conspicuous investment by an imperial (and colonial) state. The Russian state, transformed by extensive administrative and legal reforms, was decisively modernized throughout the nineteenth century. This modernization involved, among other things, the creation of an increasingly effective propaganda apparatus. Art, culture, and science were then directly subsidized by the state through increasingly powerful institutions more and more linked to the state itself. I refer to the academies of fine arts and universities that lived more symbiotically with the state than ever before. The significant increase in salaries, for example, allowed university professors to be able to devote themselves to research even without possessing their own funds. This is something that can undoubtedly be regarded as a remarkable achievement. At the same time, this also shows the vulnerability of the new state-controlled academy: the twentieth century would show how dangerous such a symbiosis could be in the world of "-isms."

For a scholar of the 2020s, the nineteenth-century situation is both inspiration and memento. An effective and well-funded academic world has impressive potential, but if too dependent on political entities, it can also very easily become a treacherous tool of propaganda.

Chapter 2

Lenin, Hitler, Stalin
Anticlericalism, the Blood of Liberators, and Imperialism

Fig. 20: Explosion of the Cathedral of Christ the Saviour, Moscow, December 5, 1931.

On October 5, 1931, Moscow residents heard two powerful explosions that shook the gloomy city. It was the beginning of the 1930s, a time of great terror, when millions more innocents were about to fall victim to a new regime, and no one probably wanted to ask what was going on. When the smoke disappeared, however, everything was crystal clear: the Soviets had blown up the Cathedral of Christ the Saviour, one of the prides of the Romanov Empire [Fig. 20]. This was no surprise; anti-clericalism was built into the DNA of the Bolshevik Soviet Union. But the destruction of the Cathedral of Christ the Saviour was intended to demonstrate something else: the USSR wanted to distance itself from the tsarist imperialist policies that the cathedral embodied. A year earlier, the same fate had befallen the Alexander Nevsky Cathedral in Tbilisi. The new regime had begun to rewrite history by dynamite and by stone. But had change really come?

Utopia in Power and the End of an Empire?

After the so-called October Socialist Revolution in 1917, all the subtle (and sometimes overt) signs pointed to this rewriting of history. The rhetoric of tsarist Russia's successor, the Soviet Union, changed dramatically. The new socialist state certainly did not want to build on its imperialist past and swiftly ended the First World War by drawing on the rhetoric of the spirit of Marxist doctrine to rewrite the historical motivation for going to war, which was now revised as a clash between bourgeoisie interests and those of the innocent and exploited proletarians. At the official level, therefore, imperialism was considered an instrument of the exploitation of the working class and was strictly rejected. It would, of course, be interesting to reflect on whether this was in fact the case, and to what extent Lenin's version of the doctrine of "world revolution," which was so popular in the early years of the emerging USSR, was really opposed to the previous tsarist imperialism. But that is a subject too broad to address here.[1] However, the idea of systematically rejecting imperialism on a rhetorical level, even at times when the USSR had long since emerged as an empire, was maintained. This is exampled in the texts of the art historian Mikhail Babenchikov (1890–1957). As late as 1944, Babenchikov was still criticizing

---

[1] On the issue, see e.g., M. R. Beissinger, "Soviet Empire as 'Family Resemblance'," *Slavic Review* 65, no. 2, (2006): 294–303; Y. Slezkine, "Imperialism as the Highest Stage of Socialism," *Russian Review* 59, no. 2, (2000): 227–34.

the imperialist and colonialist policies of the tsars on the territory of conquered or annexed states:

> All of this was a direct result of Tsarist colonial policy. Tsarism, in the words of Comrade I. V. Stalin, restricted and sometimes simply abolished local schools, theatres or educational institutions in order to keep the masses in the dark. Tsarism repressed any initiative of the best people of the local population, and eventually killed any activity of the people near the land.[2]

The criticism of colonialism and imperialism has become one of the Bolshevik regime's refrains over the years. It must be admitted, however, that for most of the 1920s and 1930s the USSR, after actively seeking to regain lost imperial provinces such as Georgia, Armenia, and Ukraine, concentrated primarily on "domestic" policy and seemingly abandoned imperial ambitions. On a pragmatic level, this was due, to the great difficulties in building the communist state. After the years of civil war, the Soviet state was unstable, and it took years before a real internal order was found. At the same time, the strategy of the early years of the USSR was not to intervene the agendas of other states. The signs of a return to Russian imperialism were not felt until 1939. Then, after the occupation of Poland, and the 1939 non-aggression agreement between Nazi Germany and the USSR—known as the Ribbentrop-Molotov Pact—the first steps of a new colonial policy were taken. However, these were immediately blocked by the outbreak of World War II.

In the first two decades of the Soviet regime, we can say that the imperial past of the Tsarist Empire was systematically criticized in the official discourse. This would probably suffice to explain the radical detachment of neo-Byzantine representation (and Byzantine studies) from Soviet politics.

---

2 M. Babenchikov, *Народное декоративное искусство Закавказья и его мастера* [National Decorative Arts of the Transcaucasian Region and Its Masters] (Moscow: Gosudarstvennoe architekturnoe izdatel'stvo, 1948), 14.

Byzantium and its visual echoes had been used and studied for decades as a precursor to the Romanov Empire, so it had no place in the Bolshevik paradise of the working people. In reality, the reason for this disconnect was much deeper: for the country's extremely anti-clerical Bolshevik leadership, standing on the philosophical foundations of atheist Marxism-Leninism, references to Byzantium, the Christian empire, as the forerunner of the Soviet Union, were hardly acceptable.[3] It is not surprising, then, that in the first years after the October Revolution many Russian Byzantinists had to flee. One of them was the abovementioned Nikodim Kondakov, but also younger students such as his pupil and future leading figure of Byzantine studies André Grabar (1896–1990). Others who remained in Russia were more or less persecuted, such as Dimitry Ajnalov (1862–1939). Such treatment was, of course, also due to the fact that Russian Byzantinists were—as demonstrated in the previous chapter—particularly close to the tsarist regime. The symbolic, visual, and scientific break from the neo-Byzantine past was perfectly logical: the aversion to the medieval past, evident in the historiography of these years, was not surprising at all.

Complicating this situation, especially in the early 1920s, was the position of the Soviet Union which was not yet the ideological and cultural monolith it would become in the following years. For example, the reception of medieval religious painting on panel—the celebrated "icon"—became an extremely popular artistic inspiration in the very early years after the October Revolution. In this case, it was, of course, primarily an aesthetic taste that justified this situation. In fact, since the early twentieth century, "icon" painting had fascinated modernist artists who made it one of the identifying elements of the Russian avant-garde. It should suffice to recall the work of Kazimir Malevich (1879–1935), one of the most important artists in this regard, who regularly referred

---

3 D. V. Pospielovsky, *A History of Soviet Atheism in Theory, and Practice, and the Believer, Volume 1: A History of Marxist-Leninist Atheism and Soviet Anti-Religious Police* (New York: Palgrave, 1987).

to medieval Russian painting in his work. This is particularly impressive when we consider one of his most conceptual works, namely the black square on white background. In 1915, at the last Futurist exhibition, it was displayed in the upper corner of the exhibition room, i.e. in the so-called "krasnyj ugol," a place where "icons" are traditionally placed in Russian family houses.[4] Nevertheless, the uses of the past were accepted in official circles only in the context of a reinterpretation that respected the intellectual and ideological canons of the USSR.

If we go back to critical history, we can then see that while in the 1920s no significant changes were yet felt, during the 1930s everything shifted, and the writing of history (and art history) became a way of evaluating the past from a Marxist perspective. This situation can be explained not only by the relative liberalism of the early 1920s but also by the timing of scholarly publications, which progress along timelines that are not always so swift. During those years, Soviet censorship experienced an impressive (and repressive) development. The rhetoric and concepts promoted in scholarly texts progressively changed. This is particularly evident in the writings of Nikolai Brunov (1898–1971), a scholar of the new generation. Trained in Moscow in the years immediately following the revolution, he became professor at the Moscow Institute of Architecture in 1934. In 1935, while studying the history of Byzantine architecture, he began his essay with a direct quote from Karl Marx: "Constantinople is the Eternal City, it is the Rome of the East. It is the place where Western civilization merges with Oriental barbarism under the rule of the Greek emperors…(Marx)."[5]

---

4 Foletti, *From Byzantium to Holy Russia*, 120–70; Taroutina, *The Icon and the Square*.

5 N. Brunov, *Очерки по истории архитектуры: в трех томах: Том 2: Греция. Рим. Византия* [Essays on the History of Architecture: In 3 Volumes. Issue 2: Greece. Rome. Byzantium] (Moscow: Academia, 1937), 11–12.

The general perspective of his reasoning was explicitly based on the official ideology of the USSR. Theoretically, of course, Brunov's writing could be seen as a way to overcome the regime's censorship, but the continuation of the text makes it clear how much the scholar let the Soviet *forma mentis* permeate all his thinking:

> The Byzantine Empire is a feudal, theocratic, strictly centralized monarchy, which in many ways resembles Oriental despotism. ...The feudal Byzantine Empire is, however, the direct successor of the slave-owning Roman Empire, in which the process of feudalisation in the fourth century led to the reincarnation of its economy and social foundations. ...In Byzantium, all areas of cultural activity were strictly subordinated to religion, which is typical of the feudal worldview.[6]

Brunov's text corresponds little to what one would expect from a scholar seeking objectivity: instead, the way he talks about the past reveals his biased point of view. The moralizing and anachronistic tone was indeed characteristic of the Marxist critique of history. The reader can also clearly perceive the author's (and the new regime's) distance from the past. Thus, in contemporary URSS's texts, Byzantium becomes what it was in Enlightenment mythology: a place of depravity and corruption.[7] The Byzantine, medieval, or Christian past was unacceptable to the new regime for a variety of reasons, and it is not surprising that the new direction of the country, which is entirely oriented towards a "better tomorrow," very firmly distanced itself from it. This is undoubtedly evidenced

---

6 Brunov, *Очерки по истории архитектуры*.

7 I refer for example to the famous sentence by Charles Louis de Secondat, Baron de La Brède et de Montesquieu (1689–1755): "[Byzance] n'est pas plus qu'un tissu de révolte, de seditions et de perfidies [(Byzantium) is no more than a tissue of revolt, sedition and perfidy]." Ch.-L. de Secondat Montesquieu, *Considérations sur les causes de la grandeur des Romains et de leur decadence* (Paris: A. Pougin, 1838), 179.

Fig. 21: Postcard with St. Michael's Golden-Domed Monastery, Kyiv, 1890–1905. Photo courtsey of the Library of Congress.

by the destruction of the material memory of this past. At the beginning of this chapter, I mentioned the destruction of neo-Byzantine temples in Moscow and Tbilisi. However, many other buildings suffered the same fate. One of the most tragic losses was the destruction of the twelfth-century Monastery of St. Michael's with the Golden Domes in Kiev, including most of its breath-taking mosaic decorations [Fig. 21].[8]

In sum, what happened in the early years of Bolshevik power was a progressive but radical change of orientation in the perception and use of the Byzantine past: the continuity of ideas that worked perfectly in the world of the last Romanovs had become an unbearable thought for the USSR. Byzantium, which had been a founding part of the nineteenth-century history of the Russian Empire, was now an ungrateful entity, a thing to be ashamed of in the country where (a supposed)

---

8 Hewryk, *The Lost Architecture of Kiev*.

proletarian utopia was now in power. Through them, the Byzantine world was seen as colonial, religious, and feudal—it was labelled with all the words that were perceived as outright blasphemies in the Soviet world.

The "Great Patriotic War": A Profound Shock

All the more surprising is the fundamental break in the rhetoric of the Soviet Empire concerning the medieval and Christian past that came with the Second World War. The German aggression in the summer of 1941, and the months of heavy losses that followed, caused fundamental trauma to the collective Soviet (and Russian) identity. The Wehrmacht's advance was only stopped deep in the rear—at the gates of Moscow, Leningrad, and in the very heart of Stalingrad—at the cost of a terrible loss of life. Some twenty-seven million casualties occurred on the Soviet side and millions more, including the millions of Jews, were murdered by the occupying forces.[9] Such a bleak situation led the USSR to radically change its internal policy. After the "internationalization" of the 1920s and the "Russification" of the second decade of Soviet rule, the empire discovered its weakness in the 1930s in regional responses to the "national" question. These were exploited by Adolf Hitler, especially in the Baltic republics and Ukraine. Nazi propaganda promised these nations independence in exchange for their support in the fight against the USSR. In Ukraine, for example, given the tragic attempt at autonomy in the early 1920s, this rhetoric was, to some extent, successful and, indeed, a section of the population openly supported the Nazi administration and army as its liberators.

---

9 Without wishing to enter into a very thorny subject here, it is only fair, for the sake of historical honesty, to mention that the local population also participated in the violence against the Jews. See e.g., T. Snyder, *Bloodlands: Europe Between Hitler and Stalin* (New York: Basic, 2010).

The Soviet authorities also realized that Hitler's Germany had made considerable use of the religious question in its efforts to win over Soviet citizens: the orthodox church had in fact been violently persecuted in the years prior to the world conflict. Logically, as part of propaganda in the conquered territories, the Nazi administration opened churches, allowed liturgies to be celebrated, freed priests, and even distributed holy pictures in the form of printed icons—it is an interesting aside to note that these propagandistic Orthodox holy pictures were printed in Prague, at the Kondakov Institute. This was an organization led mostly by white Russian émigrés which focused on the study of Byzantine art. The members of the institute were probably unaware of where the pictures were going, but it brought them considerable economic income, thanks to which they survived the war.[10] It should be added that even a part of the Orthodox clergy in the territories conquered by the Wehrmacht, more or less, explicitly decided to cooperate with the German administration.

In response to this situation, and more generally to Nazi propaganda in the occupied territories, Stalin and the Politburo decided on a radical change of course, at least at the official level. This was manifested both in the liberalization of religious observance and in the promotion of the national sentiments of the individual Soviet republics. Both were, of course, to be used in favour of war propaganda.[11] Officially, this change was explained, among other things, by the fact that in the weeks and months following the Nazi invasion, the Orthodox Church, sorely tried by the occupiers, took the side of the USSR. For those familiar with Stalin's policies and the conditions in the Kremlin, however, it is hard to believe that this "patriotic" activity of the Orthodox Church in the early

---

10 Foletti and Palladino, *Byzantium or Democracy?*.

11 See e.g., great synthesis: A. Roccucci, "Le tournant de la politique religieuse de Staline : Pouvoir soviétique et Église orthodoxe de 1943 à 1945," *Cahiers du monde russe* 50, no. 4 (2009): 671–98; Merritt Miner, *Stalin's Holy War*.

years of the war qualified sufficiently to explain Stalin's next decision, which was an utterly unprecedented action taken in 1943. The ruler of the USSR had the leaders of the Russian Orthodox Church brought to his office—a move which notoriously terrified them because they believed they were being taken away to be executed. To their immeasurable surprise, however, Stalin allowed them to elect a new patriarch of the Russian Orthodox Church. Moreover, after decades of persecution, the liturgy could once again be freely celebrated, and the church received unexpected material resources. The Russian Orthodox Church had not had a patriarch since 1925, when Patriarch Tikhon (1917–1925), who was persecuted by the regime, died, and Peter Krutizky (1925–1936), the *locum tenens*, or temporary representative, was executed in 1936. Stalin's decision was all the more significant and astonishing.

The explanation proposed by the Italian historian Adriano Roccucci is essential to this book. Roccucci argues that already by 1943 Stalin was, in fact, aware of the very likely victory over Hitler and the equally likely future imperialist expansion of the Soviet Union, not only in the former territories of tsarist Russia but also in the Balkans. In his conception, the Moscow patriarchate was to become an instrument for consolidating communist power in the newly occupied states, united through their Orthodox faith. In other words, Stalin decided to use the church for imperialist purposes, and *de facto* reiterated the tsarist strategy described in the previous chapter. In 1943, then, we see a radical change of direction in the way the Soviet state (and Stalin in particular) dealt with the religious question. With only slight exaggeration, we can say that Hitler's invasion and Nazi propaganda confirmed for Stalin—who had also incidentally studied in his youth at the Russian seminary in Tbilisi—the enormous potential of the "cooperation" between throne and altar.

However, it would be superficial to think that these changes in direction were merely a reaction to the war situation. Indeed, Stalin's decision must have been ripening for some time before the war: from the very first days after the Nazi invasion, both the "national" medievalism and religious

Fig. 22: A scene from the film by
Sergei Eisenstein "Alexander Nevsky," 1938.

heritage began to return to the propaganda scene of the
Soviet Union. Both of these concepts were to play an important role in the initially desperate attempt to reverse the fate
of the military conflict and then to prepare for future imperial
developments. The figure of Alexander Nevsky also returned
to the scene, literally. He became the Russian hero in the
battles against the Teutonic Order, i.e. "German," enemies
in Sergei Eisenstein's (1893–1948) celebrated eponymously
titled film which received great accolades in 1941. The film
had been prepared for screening as early as 1938 to reinforce patriotic sentiments, proving that Stalin was aware of
the potential of "medieval" propaganda even before the conflict began and that he was preparing for the clash with Nazi
Germany [Fig. 22]. However, because of the Ribbentrop-Molotov Pact, which made Nazi Germany and Stalin's Soviet Union
allies, the film did not widely reach cinemas until after the
German invasion in June 1941. With only slight exaggeration,
this film can be seen as the origin point of a genuine rebirth
of the cult of Alexander Nevsky, and shows the obvious desire
of the USSR's leaders, after a hiatus in the 1920s and 1930s,
to revisit the heroic medieval past. We can also conclude that
through the new medium of film, Nevsky became *de facto*

both a "cinematic icon" and a "mass saint."[12] This meant that Stalin, while allied with Nazi Germany, was watching with great interest the role nationalistic fervour had assumed in Europe and understood its potential. While he was still convinced that a confrontation with Germany could be avoided, the general secretary of the Communist Party was ahead of his time with launching the first stages of national propaganda.

In this context of a national religious renaissance, it is not surprising that medieval and especially Byzantine art also made a comeback.[13] In wartime, Viktor Lazarev (1897–1976), one of the most important Soviet art historians, was completing his monumental *History of Byzantine Painting* [Istoriya Vizantijskoj Zhivopisi]. In this text, the author attempts a qualitative assessment of individual medieval artists, with evaluation criteria evidently related to national issues. For example, according to Lazarev, and in accordance with this narrative, Theophanes the Greek, the teacher of icon painter Andrei Rublev, blossomed the moment he left the rigid Greek world and entered the truly free national Russian space:

> While the artist's personality does not reach great prominence in Byzantine art, not even in the fourteenth century, the opposite happens to individual schools. The fourteenth century is characterized by a process of crystallization of the national schools that are gradually freeing themselves from Byzantine influence.[14]

Here, Larazev is, in fact, claiming the late tsarist historiography. At the same time, the "national" medievalism of other

---

12 Navrotskaya, "Aleksandr Nevskii," 302–4.

13 I. Foletti and P. Rakitin, "Re-Inventing Late Antique and Early Medieval Armenia in WW2-Soviet Union," in *Re-Thinking Late Antique Armenia: Historiography, Material Culture, and Heritage*, ed. by A. Palladino, R. Campini, A. Moraschi, and I. Foletti (Brno: Brepols, 2023).

14 V. Lazarev, *История Византийской Живописи* [History of Byzantine Painting] (Moscow: Iskusstvo, 1947–1948), 365.

Soviet republics, such as that of Armenia, also returns to the fore. This is what we can, for example, read in the texts of Varazdat Arutjunjan (1909–2008) who wrote precisely during the war years:

> The struggle for the independence of the Armenian people, which was directed both against Arab and Byzantine rule, was headed by Prince Theodoros Rštuni, who was the ruler of Armenia in the initial period of the Arab raids. During the long struggle between the Caliphate and the Byzantine empire, each of the opponents tried to attract Armenia to their side.[15]

Following this logic, Arutjunjan considered the art produced in this period—a period which came to be called the "golden age" of Armenian architecture—as independent from both the Byzantine and Arab worlds. The overtly nationalistic tone of this passage would perhaps not be surprising in interwar Western Europe, when the question of a "national art" was a widespread debate. After decades during which the art of Armenia and of the entire Southern Caucasus had been presented by Russian art historians as provincial (and, thus, subordinate to some great empire), its suddenly unique national role and identity were unanticipated. Again, there is reason to suspect that this change in rhetoric was intended to foster an environment of "great patriotic war" in the struggle against Nazism.

Thus, in the 1940s, it seemed that the events of the war, together with the new path of the Russian Orthodoxy, would reverse the fortunes of the "Byzantine" and "medieval" past within the USSR. The result of these changes was in fact the adoption of a political strategy that unexpectedly, yet quite clearly, retained some of the key points of late nineteenth-century ideology. It could be argued, then, that the leadership of the Soviet Union during the Second World War

---

15 V. Arutjunjan, *По поводу датировки храма в Аруче* [Regarding the Dating of the Temple in Aruč] (Yerevan: Izd. Po delam arxitektury pri Sovmine ArmSSR, 1946), 3.

returned to the traditional tzarist concepts mentioned above: to autocracy as presented by Stalin, to Orthodoxy, and to the peoples of the Soviet Union.

Marking New Territories

Meanwhile, Soviet troops, with significant economic and military assistance from Western Allies, began to make their victorious journey to Berlin. Before that, however, Europe was divided between the Western Allies and the Soviet Union at the so-called Yalta Conference in February 1945. As Stalin likely suspected would be the case in 1943, he had, indeed, become the aging ruler of a vast empire, including satellite countries far beyond the USSR, by the end of the war. He had ascended to the pinnacle of power. It remains a paradox of history that even during the war, the Soviet Union continued to suffer terrible purges and major military miscalculations that increased the number of casualties, for which Stalin himself was on more than one occasion directly responsible. Another tragic chapter is undoubtedly the criminalization and subsequent harsh persecution of all prisoners of war who fell into the hands of the Wehrmacht.[16] In addition, the Soviet NKVD units were directly responsible for some of the casualties, who with incredible brutality "boosted the morale" of their own deployed soldiers by "shooting them in the back" if they retreated before the enemy.

Notwithstanding these atrocities, the Soviet Union was perceived as having made a decisive contribution to the fall of Nazi Germany, and, objectively, the country's contribution to the war effort had been truly outstanding. The loss of human life was enormous. In some battles, such as at Moscow, Leningrad, and Stalingrad, casualties numbered in the millions.

---

16 On the perception of war from the perspective of "ordinary people," see for example the very stimulating collection *Combattre, survivre, témoigner: Expériences soviétiques de la Seconde Guerre mondiale*, ed. E. Koustova (Strasbourg: Presses universitaires de Strasbourg, 2020).

As already mentioned, it cannot be forgotten that no small part of the casualties on the Soviet side, especially in what is now Ukraine, were caused by the genocidal agenda of the SS. It is important to recall that it was the Soviet army that first exposed the Nazi genocidal crimes in Ukraine (and also the extermination camps in Poland) before the end of the war. I recall in this sense the writings of the military correspondent and arguably one of the most talented Russian writers of the twentieth century, Vasily Grossman (1905–1964), who was an eyewitness to these revelations: Grossmann was among the first to enter Treblinka and the first to recount what had been contrived for years in this camp. In addition to newspaper articles and short journalistic texts, he devoted part of his greatest literary work to the war time including the first ever monograph about the extermination camps.[17]

Ironically, this horrific bloodshed became an argument for Stalin and the USSR leadership to further expand the empire, with the pretext for the military presence of Soviet troops in these countries being to protect the satellite states from further war and threats. Together with the Western Allies, it was also to monitor the situation in Germany, which led to the creation of the German Democratic Republic (DDR) and guaranteed the USSR a military presence in that region as well. Officially, the Yalta division of Europe was to be a tool to keep the peace, with strong victorious empires protecting the weaker ones and an aggressive Germany neutralized. In reality, however, this division of Europe laid the foundations for the Cold War.[18] In 1945, the Soviet Union expanded from Siberia to the Baltic, while other states, including Czechoslovakia, Hungary, Poland, and Romania, gradually became satellites of the superpower.

---

17 V. Grossman, *Life and Fate* (New York: Vintage, 2006); V. Grossman, *L'inferno di Treblinka* (Milan: Adelphi, 2010).

18 Berthon and Potts, *Warlords*; D. Wolff, "Stalin's Postwar Border-Making Tactics," *Cahiers du monde russe* 52, no. 2-3 (2011): 273–91.

Fig. 23: Boris Iofan, Soviet pavilion at the *Exposition Internationale des Arts et Techniques dans la Vie Moderne*, with the sculpture of Worker and Kolkhoz Woman, Vera Mukhina, Paris, 1937.

Fig. 24: German pavilion at the
*Exposition Internationale des Arts et
Techniques dans la Vie Moderne*, Paris, 1937.

This was reflected in the visual representation of the war victors in the newly "conquered" territories. Architecture and art had been officially at the service of the working people since the beginning of the USSR, and this trend became even stronger in the post-war period.[19] After the first modernist phase in the 1920s—when, for example, an architect such as Le Corbusier was invited to the USSR—in the 1930s, very conservative and grandiose architecture became normative in the Soviet Union. This architecture was characterized by monumental proportions and a decidedly classicizing morphology that evoked both ancient Roman and Nazi models [Figs. 23–24].[20] Such an architectural lexicon had developed chiefly in public monuments—such as buildings related to the promotion of the Communist Party, courthouses, or hotels—but had also been used systematically for dwellings. During the pre-war years, Moscow was radically transformed under the impetus of this new style which made it one of the most monumental cities in the world. The city's new look was composed of truly impressive buildings whose monumental cubature made human beings feel like only a tiny, almost oppressed, element of how the country was being newly represented. For the USSR, such transformations, which were also widespread in many countries in the interwar period, had two distinct meanings. On the one hand, they participated in Stalin's project of building a new man—the Soviet man—while, at the same time, they also helped promote a

---

19 This topic is too large to deal with here. V. Buchli, *An Archaeology of Socialism* (Oxford: Routledge, 2000), is very stimulating for understanding the relationship between regime and architecture. The author shows the extent to which the regime used architecture, including the construction of housing, to enter the private space of Soviet citizens. Heather D. Dehaan's study, *Stalinist City Planning*, uses the example of Nizhny Novgorod to show the regime's construction of public space. Dehaan, *Stalinist City Planning*.

20 See e.g., Paperny, *Architecture in the Age of Stalin: Culture Two*; Udovicki-Selb, "Between Modernism and Socialist Realism.

Fig. 25: War memorial to honour students and workers of
Moscow State University lost during the Great Patriotic War.
In the background stands the university building, the highest
of the Seven Sisters—Stalin's skyscrapers built between 1947
and 1957. Photo courtesy of D. Kyndrová. Used with permission.

visual representation of the regime's imperialist ambitions,
rivalling symbolizations of other totalitarian systems during
these years.

In the first years of the post-war period (1947–1953), a
project was carried out in Moscow that became characteristic of Stalinist architecture and the growing ambitions of
the USSR: the construction of seven skyscrapers called the
"Seven Sisters" [Fig. 25]. These towering buildings were
intended to present the glory of the proletariat and to mate-
rialize the power of the Soviet Union in public space through
their size and iconography. The project included buildings for
the Ministry of the Interior and Moscow University, as well as
hotels and houses for Soviet writers. American skyscrapers
were an undoubted source of inspiration for these buildings in
terms of size, but the classical style, full of proletarian motifs,
contributed greatly to their different visual appearance.

Fig. 26: Boris Iofan, Vladimir Shchuko, and Vladimir
Helfreich, Palace of the Soviets, project, 1933.
Photo courtesy of Alexander Koyagin.

At the birth of this monumental urban project was another, even more ambitious building. This was the so-called Palace of Soviets, a skyscraper that was to be the tallest building in the city, dominated by a gigantic statue of Lenin [Fig. 26]. However, another aspect is crucial to this text: the Palace of Soviets was to replace the Temple of Christ the Saviour, which, as mentioned in the introduction to this chapter, was blown up on December 5, 1931. In the 1930s, a time of the most brutal religious persecution within the USSR, the revival of Orthodoxy described above was still unimaginable. Even in this period, however, Soviet power played with ideas of discontinuity (destruction) and continuity (preservation) with the previous world. Thus, the Palace of Soviets was not only used as proof of the definitive victory of communist ideology, but also as proof that the USSR was the rightful geopolitical successor to the Tsarist Empire, including its expansionist ambitions. However, war and development problems ultimately prevented the construction of the Palace of Soviets.

Even without this landmark, the "Seven Sisters" became the iconic buildings dominating the Moscow cityscape. The models and visual concepts that developed in Moscow began to spread from the USSR and were, at first glance, very different from those used by tsarist propaganda. On closer inspection, however, the way in which architecture in particular was used clearly follows the imperialist tradition of the nineteenth century. Copies of the Seven Sisters were created—for example in Bucharest, Prague, and Warsaw [Figs. 27–28]. Similar, though smaller, buildings can be found for example in Sofia, Rostov, and as far as Beijing. It is worth remembering that, after the Yalta's Conference, the majority of central European countries were put under the "protection" of the USSR. In the years following the World War II, these countries became—more or less democratically—communist and entered an ideological communion with the USSR.

What followed was a very violent process of Sovietiza-tion—with the creation of concentration camps, public trials against enemies of the people, executions, expropriations, etc.—including the adoption of the Soviet proletarian mytho-

Fig. 27: Hotel International, Prague, 1952–1956.
Photo courtesy of Simon Legner.

logy. According to the official interpretation, the composition and iconography of the "copies" of the "Seven Sisters" were intended to glorify the working people. However, I am convinced that, as was the case in the nineteenth century, this was also a clear way of marking of each nations' sphere of influence. It is beyond the scope of this book to address the question of how concretely the Soviet architectural ideas

were "exported" to those states which came to be described as "satellites" of the USSR. It is evident, though, that the operation was coordinated from Moscow and accepted—very likely with enthusiasm—by members of the Communist Party in the newly conquered territories. Stalinist architects succeeded in creating a unified visual style for the new Soviet Empire and its subordinate states. Incidentally, just as the neo-Byzantine style was the obligatory visual language for sacred buildings across the empire, so the unified Soviet style throughout the USSR created a visual language promot-

Fig. 28: Palace of Culture and Science, Warsaw, 1955.
Photo courtsey of FORTEPAN / Romák Éva.

ing the glory of the proletariat. It is necessary to distinguish between the unity afforded through the centralized production of various building elements on the one hand and the conscious effort to unify the Soviet Empire on the other. It is the latter that was particularly visible in representative public buildings. The empire had, indeed, found itself a unified visual style. Just as neo-Byzantine architecture was a symbol of tsarism in the nineteenth century, Moscow's skyscrapers became both a visualization of Stalinist power and models for architectural colonization.

The Past of the Present:
The Vitreous Mosaic and Images of Power

Although the official architecture was far removed in appearance from the neo-Byzantine style of the tsarist past, in the 1940s the medieval identity returned with unprecedented force. Beyond the architecture, which in Yerevan, for example, explicitly worked with medieval Armenian morphology, echoes of the new Stalinist cultural policy can be noted above all in the techniques used in the visual arts. The medium of glass mosaics is a clear reminder of the medieval tradition. It began to appear regularly in the interiors of the skyscrapers already mentioned, as well as in several stations of the Moscow metro, which was a great bragging point for the Stalinist regime. Mosaics were created there during and after the end of World War II.

One of the most impressive examples can be found at Komsomolskaya Station, which was opened in 1952. Its iconography was inspired by Stalin's speech in November 1941. Delivered at the time of the furious retreat of Soviet troops and the seemingly inevitable victory of Nazi Germany, Stalin's goal was to rouse the Soviet army and people. His fiery speech recalled the historical leaders of the Russian Empire who led the country to great victories. He recalled their heroisms as well as the irreplaceable and no less heroic role of the entire Russian people. Stalin's speech could not have begun other than with the Middle Ages and the struggle against the Teutonic Order (framed at this time as the German knights). It is not surprising, then, that among those depicted in Komsomolskaya were figures of medieval heroes including the aforementioned Alexander Nevsky or Dmitry Donskoy.

The mosaic depicting Alexander Nevsky is worthy of a brief description: the medieval prince is depicted on a mighty white horse, holding a banner on which is depicted, in a neo-Byzantine style, the mandylion, that is, miraculous, legendary image of Christ, not made by human hands [Fig. 29]. The saint is clad in knightly armour and his figure is clearly intended to highlight the medieval and Orthodox

Fig. 29: Pavel Korin, Mosaic of Alexander Nevsky,
Komsomolskaja Station, Moscow, 1951–1952.
Photo courtesy of N. Rakitina, 2023.
Used with permission.

roots of Russian culture and heroism. However, there is another striking aspect: the banner with the image of the mandylion dominates the whole composition. The adopted style, neo-Byzantine, emphasized by the golden background and the iconography, intentionally connected and referred to medieval Russian culture. This hypothesis is confirmed by the figure of Dimitry Donskoy, who is depicted in a very similar manner to that of Alexander Nevsky: in his case, too, the central image of the composition is the mandylion. What the images seem to emphasize is the cumulative importance of the Orthodox and medieval tradition upstream of the victory in the "Great Patriotic War." The stories of Russian victories—that began with Alexander Nevsky and Dimitry Donskoy and end at Komsomolskaya Station with Joseph Stalin's victory in World War II—are, therefore, unthinkable without the religious and cultural traditions of the pre-modern world.

In this sense, the choice of the representing the mandylion in the composition was also an important one. It was, in fact, one of the most adored images in the Orthodox world to which special powers were imputed at all layers of medieval religiosity, especially during crises and wars. Thanks to the mandylion, Constantinople had been saved repeatedly during the wars that had threatened it over the centuries. It was believed that the miraculous image had an immense power of protection, granting victory to those who worshipped it. Presenting it in the context of a celebration of the USSR's wartime victory must, I believe, also be read in this context: implicitly considering that the power of Orthodox images had actively participated in the war effort. It was a return to the past-as-power.

The situation was in this sense even more interesting—especially if one considers the figure of the author of the metro mosaics who was decorated for this feat with the Stalin Prize, in 1954. Pavel Korin (1892–1967) was a restorer, painter, and mosaicist who has a truly extraordinary biography. He was born in the village of Palekh, in one of the last villages where "icons" were still being produced in the traditional way at the end of the nineteenth century; his father was himself an "icon" painter. Korin had been trained before the revolution in one of the painting schools promoted in the early twentieth century by Nikodim Kondakov and the Tsar Nicolas I (1894–1917)—mentioned in the previous chapter—to save the ancient art of Orthodox painting on panel.[21] After the revolution, Korin was active as an icon painter and restorer, but he also started to paint portraits, and was even greatly admired by the likes of Maxim Gorky. After Gorky's death, having lost his support, Korin was harshly criticized for his style, which was too different to the dogma of socialist realism. Marginalized, he devoted himself mainly to restoration, but also produced a series of realistic portraits. He then began to deal with the subject of Russian heroes, particularly Alexander Nevsky—as early as 1942, after Stalin's speech, but especially after the publication and popularity of Eisenstein's film—and also of Dmitry Donskoy. In his person, the nineteenth-century history of neo-medieval art (neo-Russian or neo-Byzantine) merged in an incredible way with Soviet experience. Trained before the revolution, Korin had all the technical and iconographic skills to deal with Russian heroism. At the same time, he was a person loyal to Soviet power, who accepted and integrated part of the social-ist-realist canon.

This biography shows us how much—extending beyond appearances or pretences—the Soviet establishment had in its bosom people who thoroughly understood the visual strategies of the "ancient regimes" from which it sought to be inspired. Korin was also a figure capable of making compromises with the regime—he was the author of a portrait of Marshal Zhukov in 1945 and had also been a drawing teacher for Beria's children—while maintaining his Orthodox identity. The return to the past was possible both at the level of form

---

21 For the situation in Palekh and for the initiatives of Kondakov see N. P. Kondakov, *The Current State of Russian Folk Icon Painting*, trans. by M. Khakhanova and S. Melker, ed. I. Foletti, A. Palladino, and Z. Urbanová (Brno: Viella, 2022).

and content, but also at the level of a deeper cultural sub-stratum that the thirty years of Soviet power had failed to completely eradicate. The crisis due to the war showed the importance of such patterns for the country's identity.

Conclusion

The words of Stalin's speech and their subsequent materi-alization in mosaic decoration during the Second World War created a new story of Russian and Soviet history. Medieval heritage, Byzantine tradition, and their *revival* in the nine-teenth century reappeared in the visual rhetoric of the post-war Soviet Empire.

The choice to build a Soviet palace on the site where the Cathedral of Christ the Saviour once stood, the way imperial architecture was used to colonize satellite states, the return of the mosaic in post-war triumphalist self-presentation, as well as the Orthodox (and Byzantine-nationalist) revival, all demonstrate how the Soviet system—at the latest after the Second World War and despite a sharp breaking point in rhet-oric—adopted some of the key identity elements of the Tsa-rist regime. The cult of the autocrat was, of course, replaced by the cult of the party (and its leaders or leader), but the basic features of this specific mode of thinking persisted.

Chapter 3

Luzhkov, Putin, and the Dream
of the Return of Empire

When I asked a friend from Moscow, now an expatriate in Georgia, to explain how Russia could have fallen so quickly into Vladimir Putin's authoritarian regime after the fall of the USSR sometime in the early 2000s, his response was unequivocal: "It was the 1990s, it was a jungle!" The stories he told me afterwards helped me to understand at least a little why the demand for a "firm hand" was so great after 2000.

Fig. 30: Moscow, around 2000. Photo courtesy of D. Kyndrová. Used with permission.

Fig. 31: Demonstration by Russian Communists on the anniversary of the Bolshevik Revolution. In the background stands one of the Seven Sisters—Kotelnicheskaya Embankment Building, Moscow, November 7, 2001. Photo courtesy of D. Kyndrová. Used with permission.

In the 1990s, household savings were almost completely wiped out and inflation had led to elderly people—"senior citizens" who had given so much to their society and country—begging on the streets and starving to death. I cannot forget the begging grandmothers I used to meet on every corner during my first visits to Moscow. All rules had, it seemed, disappeared from the country [Fig. 30]. The practice of borrowing a sum of money from an acquaintance, a fraction of which could be used to pay a hired assassin who then murdered the acquaintance of the person in question and relieved them of the obligation to repay the loan, was, at the least, said to be commonly practiced. The market for the profession of assassin for hire was reportedly so saturated after the breakup of the elite military units that an assassination for hire cost about $2,000. In the resulting chaos, society became radicalized, allowing nostalgia for the previous regime, neo-Nazis, Stalinists, and religious fanatics to coexist [Fig. 31]. The trauma of this period, duly fed by the resulting Putin propaganda, can be seen as one of the key reasons for Russia's current imperialism.

To better understand the roots of the current situation, in this chapter I would like to address the most recent period—that which corresponds to the last thirty years of Russian history, and not only the artistic aspects. I will, first of all, summarize the salient facts of politics with a special focus on economics in the 1990s. Secondly, I will present the reconstruction of the Cathedral of Christ the Saviour from its much-discussed rebuilding in the nineties to the times when it was included in the celebrated performance of the punk feminist rock band Pussy Riot in 2012. Finally, I would like to return to the building with which this book began, the 2020 Russian Armed Forces Cathedral. The concept of this church can be seen as the emblem of current imperialist ideology, an ideology that, at all levels, refers more or less to imaginary pasts to justify the present.

The Collapse of an Empire or "Shock Therapy?"

At the beginning, there was no indication that post-Soviet Russia would soon become an aggressive empire. When the Soviet Union collapsed in 1991, one chapter of imperialist tendencies seemed to have ended.[1] [Fig. 32] The empire collapsed for many reasons, but economic issues and ethnic tensions played a key role in the whole process. The collapse of the empire was accompanied by the emergence of new

---

1 A huge number of texts have been devoted to the fall of the USSR. See, for example, M. Beissinger, "Nationalism and the Collapse of Soviet Communism," *Contemporary European History* 18, no. 3 (2008): 331–47. For more on nationalist tensions, see A. Brown, *The Gorbachev Factor* (Oxford: Oxford Academic Press, 1997). On the political role played by Mikhail Gorbachev in the collapse of the USSR, see C. I. Miller, *The Struggle to Save the Soviet Economy: Mikhail Gorbachev and the Collapse of the USSR* (Chapel Hill: University of North Carolina Press, 2016).

Fig. 32: Removal of Lenin's monument, Uzhhorod, 1991.
Photo courtesy of D. Kyndrová. Used with permission.

"nation-states," based on no small amount of nationalism. In the first chapter, it was possible to conclude that Polish nationalism was one of the triggers of Russian imperialism, but in this case, it is evident that communist imperialism was one of the main drivers of the formation of nationalist sentiments throughout the country, from Georgia to Ukraine and Kazakhstan to Armenia. Indeed, by its very nature, the Soviet Empire suppressed separatist and nationalist tendencies in the territories it had seized in the past, but this, especially in some parts of the USSR, had quite the opposite effect. Repressed local identities were strengthened by persecution.

In the Russian Federation, born from the ashes of the USSR, there was a period of incredible chaos, a large-scale financial fraud, and social crisis. This crisis had been caused by both the destabilization of the political system but, perhaps even more substantially, by the "liberal reforms" promoted by Boris Yeltsin (1931–2007). Yeltsin had been elected president of Russia with a hero's reputation, as he had defended the parliament with his own body during the coup against Mikhail Gorbachev in the summer of 1991. Once in power, Yeltsin was given, for the duration of one year, carte blanche by the state Duma to carry out the reforms necessary to leave behind the communist planned economy and transition the country to a free market economy. Mikhail Gorbachev (1931–2022), the last head of the USSR and the father of the Perestroika—that is the "restructuring," a complex change in the Soviet economic system—viewed his goal as a gradual transformation of the country into a Scandinavian-style social democracy. Yeltsin, for his part, promoted radical liberalization on models tried out in the 1980s, for example in Bolivia and in Great Britain. The basic idea, based on the economic research of Milton Friedman (1912–2006) and his "Chicago School," was to rapidly privatize the country by transferring its wealth into private hands. In parallel, the state was to minimalize its economic interventions and, generally, the services provided by the state itself. The desired situation was to leave the market as free as possible. It was then assumed that this would produce a new equilibrium (and prosperity) in the country devastated by decades of communist rule and planned economy.

The first results of this "shock therapy" administered to the country following advice from, for example, Jeffrey Sachs (1954), then a professor at Harvard University, were devastating.[2] Freed from state control at a rapid pace, the country's economy experienced dramatic moments with galloping inflation, but also with purchases of entire slices of the market in a very profitable gamble, unscrupulous speculators pounced on the country, enriching themselves at the expense of the

---

2 On the Russian "shock therapy" see e.g., S. Rosefielde, "Premature Deaths: Russia's Radical Economic Transition in Soviet Perspective," *Europe-Asia Studies* 53 (2001): 1159–76. A journalistic but well documented synthesis is the book by N. Klein, *The Shock Doctrine: The Rise of Disaster Capitalism* (New York: Picador, 2008). Sachs offered his reading of the facts on several occasions, downplaying his own role but acknowledging the weight of the Bush and Clinton administrations in the crisis that devastated Russia see Sachs, "Russia's Tumultuous Decade."

population. The immediate results of the change were devastating economically: in the various waves of unrestrained privatization, whose purpose was often to maximize profits in minimal time, 80 percent of agricultural firms and more than seventy thousand factories went bankrupt during the years of the Yeltsin era (1991–1999). This caused a dramatic social situation: if in 1989 there were two million Russians living below the poverty line (less than four dollars a day) by the mid-1990s their number had increased to ca. seventy-two million. Alcoholism, traditionally blamed on the communist regime increased by 100 percent in 1994, while the suicide rate quadrupled. Nearly three million orphans poured into the streets, while "middle class" families lost their life savings, which were devoured by inflation of 2,600 percent in December of 1992, an all-time high. In a word, in terms of social structures, it was the apocalypse.[3] In this context, one essential element must be remembered. At the worst of the crisis, as recalled by Sachs himself:

> [The] Bush administration came in the form of tough U.S. warnings that Russia should continue to pay its debts at all costs (specifically, that a default would be met by a stoppage of vital food aid). The result was a contribution to Russia's financial destabilization at the critical period of early 1992. The International Monetary Fund is written off as a thoroughly miscast institution, not appropriate for the tasks for which it was assigned by the West. It is specifically charged with having delayed stabilization in the vital months of 1992 by its mistaken advice to the post-Soviet states to delay the introduction of national currencies. In short, the West did almost nothing to affect the outcomes for democracy and market reforms in Russia, despite all the high-minded rhetoric to the contrary.[4]

3 See e.g., the synthesis by B. Silverman and M. Yanowitch, *New Rich, New Poor, New Russia Winners and Losers on the Russian Road to Capitalism* (New York: Routledge, 2000), 47.

4 Sachs, "Russia's Tumultuous Decade."

While Sachs does not question the economic system he wanted to help establish, he acknowledges—and this is an essential fact—the role and responsibility of the United States of America and the International Monetary Fund in the rapid escalation of the Russian economic crisis, which in terms of brutality and casualties was a warlike event. With no regulations and no socio-cultural premises, privatization was a death sentence for millions of Russians aided and abetted by exterior political and economic pressure on Russian elites.

In the fall of 1993, in one of the most dramatic moments for Russia's new democracy, Yeltsin was deposed by the parliament, who were unhappy with the way presidential reforms were being carried out. The president responded by dissolving the parliament: two democratically elected institutions were in open conflict. The president accused members of parliament of being nostalgic Stalinists and called out the army, which attacked parliament on October 4. There were deaths and injuries, but the worst was to come for the new democracy in another form: although the Western press had presented the events as a victory of reform against the communist counterrevolution, the reality was much more complex, and the president had acted unconstitutionally, although the constitutionality of his decisions is, of course, still debated today.[5]

As if that were not enough, criminal organizations came to power, unofficially existing groups of criminals, the so-called "rafts in the law," who were in reality thieves living according to a criminal code that had been in place since Stalin's gulags. Then, they bullied political prisoners and enjoyed much more lenient treatment from the camp administration. It was these groups that responded most quickly to social change, as they had both financial resources and a relatively solid organizational structure—which was lacking in most other areas of social and economic life in Russia. The brutality and violence

---

5 J. T. Andrews, *When Majorities Fail: the Russian Parliament, 1990-1993* (Cambridge: Cambridge University Press, 2002), 61-65.

that accompanied this period was shocking to the post-Soviet population.[6] Moreover (and perhaps above all), after centuries of autocracy and proletarian dictatorship, the country lacked a popular vision—an accepted national ideology. A shared belief system might have pulled together the disparate parts of this loosely knit system, but with the rise of atheism a general ideological dissonance resulted. The free market could in no way replace the official doctrine that had presented the state and contributed to its cohesion for centuries.

In sum, the 1990s corresponded to a dramatic and tragic moment in Russia. Controversial economic reforms resulted in a staggering number of victims, but more importantly they created a major collective trauma which affected many others. Finally, and likewise traumatically, the blatant failure of the reforms was explained in the West by an alleged ontological inability of Russians to live in a liberal (and, therefore, democratic) system. In addition to trauma, this period also generated resentment toward the West, which had openly supported Yeltsin and his politics. And it is this resentment that is one of the keys to understanding the subsequent development of Russia where, in 1999, without democratic elections, Yeltsin was succeeded by Vladimir Putin.

The Throne and the Altar Meeting Again?

It is in the context of the economic, political, and moral crises that have taken turns in Russia since 1991 that the resurgence of Russian imperialism must be analyzed. Given what has been written in the previous chapters, it is not surprising

---

6 On this transition period, see e.g., D. M. Kotz and F. Weir, *Russia's Path from Gorbachev to Putin: The Demise of the Soviet System and the New Russia* (London: Routledge, 2007). For a critical perspective on the "Wild Nineties," see e.g., A. Edwards and R. Rabbia, "The 'Wild Nineties': Youth Engagement, Memory and Continuities between Yeltsin's and Putin's Russia," in *Youth and Memory in Europe: Defining the Past, Shaping the Future*, ed. F. Friess and N. Friess (Berlin: De Gruyter 2022), 75–83.

that this "revival" movement is intimately linked to the new role played by the Orthodox Church in the post-1991 period.

In a situation of profound dismay, indeed, the Orthodox Church, graced with the martyr's glorioIe of the Soviet years, began to regain its popularity. Indeed, it is important to remember that after the interlude of the war, with Stalin creating a more "comfortable" situation for Orthodoxy, especially since the reign of Nikita Khrushchev (1894–1971), anticlericalism and persecution of the church returned as the order of the day. As late as 1990, one of the most interesting theologians of his time, Alexander Men (1935–1990), was brutally murdered, most likely by the KGB. If in the war years the throne and the altar had found a new modus operandi, in the following years and until the end of the USSR, the coexistence of church and state was very problematic, to put it mildly. In this context, it is not surprising that a considerable part of the faithful and clerics started playing an active role in the dissident movement in the last years of the communist regime. Considering this historical backstory, what happened in the nineties is shocking: at least from the mid-1990s onwards, a new convergence and then a union of "throne and altar"—the regime of Yeltsin and Putin and the Orthodox Church—could be observed. This is all the more paradoxical when we consider the fact that the "throne" was often the direct heir of the very same forces that had persecuted the church for decades—former members of the Communist Party like Yeltsin or even of the notorious KGB like Putin. This paradox can be explained not only by a certain naiveté on the part of some members of the Orthodox Church, but also by the rhetoric of the new power following the collapse of their communist forebearers: the "throne," consisting overwhelmingly of members of the USSR nomenclature, presented itself as a successor to the tradition and authority of the tsars.

This is all the more absurd considering the fact that the new Russian leaders, emerging from the cadres of the Marxist regime who were often personally atheistic, claimed to reconnect with a deeply religious past. Such a situation is paradoxical because, despite a substantial revival of reli-

Fig. 33: Celebrations of the 200th anniversary of victory over
Napoleon in the Patriotic War of 1812, Borodino, 2012.
Photo courtesy of D. Kyndrová. Used with permission.

gious life in parishes around the country, the vast majority of
the population—including the elites—was atheist. This reality gradually led to the phenomenon known as "de-seculari-
zation," that is a gradual rise in the power of the Orthodox
Church, but without a significant increase in personal piety
[Fig. 33].[7]

In this second stage, we can say that the Orthodox
elites, personified mainly by the patriarchs of Moscow, willingly accepted the power that the new regime offered them.
Becoming loyal to a corrupt, belligerent, and often criminal
"throne," the leaders of the Orthodox church were progressively corrupted in turn (at least on a moral level) and lost
the legacy of the persecuted church, replacing it with one
of elitist corruption. What followed is what we might define

---

7 V. Karpov, "Desecularization: A Conceptual Framework," *Journal
of Church and State* 52, no. 2 (2010): 232–70, esp. 236–40.

as the concept of "public religion."[8] In the Russian context of the Yeltsin period, this notion describes a situation when religion became a type of collective identity that had nothing to do with the personal relationship of individuals to their faith. This is illustrated by the fact that in the 1990s, paradoxically, 75 percent of Russians considered themselves "Orthodox" but only 40 percent "religious." Furthermore, the vast majority did not participate in any religious practices.[9] This can be explained on purely political and "identity" grounds, since official propaganda in the same years emphasized the close link between the Orthodox Church and "ethnic Russians." Thus, the idea began to spread that every Russian was Orthodox by "nature," regardless of whether they believed in God or not. One bit of explicit evidence of this new reality—which at the same time strikes at the very heart of this volume—was undoubtedly the reconstruction of the Cathedral of Christ the Saviour in Moscow (1994–1997), a building that has accompanied us throughout this text.

The idea of rebuilding this cathedral, destroyed by the Stalinist regime, originally came from "below." The first design by the sculptor Vladimir Mokrousov (1936–2021) was created in the late 1980s during the period of perestroika.[10] A fraternity was born around it, which received permission from the city authorities to build a small chapel in memory of the destroyed cathedral. After 1994, however, the church and state authorities took control. The patriarchate, headed by Alexios II (1929–2008), dissolved the brotherhood and began

---

8 J. Casanova, "Public Religion Revisited" in *Religion, Beyond the Concept*, ed. H. de Vries (New York: Fordham University Press, 2008); J. Casanova, *Public Religions in the Modern World* (Chicago: University of Chicago Press, 1994).

9 K. Kaariainen and D. Furman, "Religiosity in Russia in the 1990s," in *Religious Transition in Russia*, ed. M. Kotiranta (Helsinki: Kikimora, 2000), 28–76.

10 K. Smith, "An Old Cathedral for a New Russia: The Symbolic Politics of the Reconstituted Church of Christ the Saviour," *Religion, State and Society* 25, no. 2 (1997): 163–75 , esp. 168–72.

a new and very ambitious construction. While the idea of building a small chapel was the result of Orthodox piety, this new project was primarily a political act. It is no coincidence that the new construction was also "blessed" by President Boris Yeltsin himself:

> Dear compatriots! With deep gratitude I greet you and among all of you I greet those who are taking up the noble mission of turning the idea of rebuilding the Cathedral of Christ the Saviour into reality. We were destined to live in a difficult time of destruction and creation, in a time of tragic confrontation between the old and the new, in times of changes in economic and political foundations. …Russia today needs the Cathedral of Christ the Saviour. It is Russia's national shrine and should be revived. With it, it will be easier for all of us to find the way to social cohesion, to create goodness and to create a life in which there is less room for sin. I wholeheartedly support your initiative, and I am sure that the Russian government and regional authorities at all levels will consider it one of the most important tasks and will help its speedy implementation.[11]

The words spoken by Yeltsin are crucial for the present volume: not only does the president present the situation as that of a kind of new foundation, but he speaks clearly of the need for the country to possess a national temple and also mentions the idea of a place with a reduced "room for sin." Such words are impressive coming from a man trained in Marxist materialism—thus in traditional atheism—and whose years in government were not characterized, as written above, by any particular "morality." Such a shift in perspective seems to be

---

11 B. Yel'cin, "Обращение президента российской федерации к членам общественного наблюдательного собрания по воссозданию Храма Христа [Address of the President of the Russian Federation to the Members of the Public Supervisory Board after the Reconstruction of the Cathedral of Christ the Saviour]," *Российская газета* [Rossiyskaya gazeta] (1994); for translation from Russian into English see Foletti, *The Cathedral of Christ the Savior*, 50.

explainable only in a very pragmatic way: with all evidence, Yeltsin wanted to use Orthodoxy for his political needs.

The situation of the church reconstruction project also shows us the speed at which the patriarchate and new regime found a happy symbiosis in breaking with the recent past. The initiative to remake the church was a genuine gesture by the believers, conceivable only in the Gorbatchev years. Snatching the initiative from the faithful and making it a political act was symptomatic of the new Russia.

This is an aspect that we can identify in all the developmental stages of the cathedral itself. The key figure during the construction was Moscow Mayor Yuri Luzhkov (1939–2019), former Communist Party executive, active in Soviet politics since the late 1970s. He was the real "patron" of the building project and raised the funds for its implementation. In the same breath, it should be added that the funds that Luzhkov accumulated for the construction of the cathedral were, to put it mildly, of problematic origin.[12] They came from the wild businesses that dominated the Russian economy at the time, and sometimes from sources directly connected to the criminal underworld. This corruption did not go unnoticed or uncriticized. Naturally, it led to open criticism from both the Orthodox faithful and liberals. However, these critical voices echoed in an empty room, ineffective and unheard. Moreover, the construction was criticized because of its high cost. In times of dramatic crisis and unprecedented poverty, with nearly half of Russia's population facing poverty—such an ambitious building was considered a sign of arrogance. The patriarchy's problematic approach was also questioned, as funds from the sale of tobacco and other commodities in a tax-free system were used to build the church.

In official rhetoric, however, the cathedral was to become a "Russian national shrine" implicitly linked, once again, to the imperial past. To this end, the new building was to take

---

12 D. N. Jensen, "The Boss: How Yuri Luzhkov Runs Moscow," *Demokratiztsiya* 8, no. 1 (2000): 83–122.

Fig. 34: Cathedral of Christ the Saviour, Moscow, 1903.
Photo courtesy of William H. Rau, Library of Congress.

on the visual form of the original [Fig. 34]. In other words, the neo-Russian (neo-Byzantine) tradition was to be restored. On a symbolic level, the situation was clear: Yeltsin's Russia wanted to visually reconnect with the visual (and ideological) legacy of the Romanovs. Only a few years later, in August 2000, the family of the last Tsar Nicholas II (1884–1917) who were murdered by the Bolsheviks, were canonized.

It might have seemed that seventy years of communism were simply to be abolished, as the Cathedral of Christ the Saviour was to demonstrate on a visual level. Indeed, from a distance the building appears identical to the previous

Fig. 35: View of the Cathedral of Christ the Saviour, 2001. Photo courtesy of D. Kyndrová. Used with permission.

one [Fig. 35]: it had a central plan and was dominated by a main dome, while four other domes were located in the four corners. As with the original, the roofs were gilded and had the famous dome shape. The façade was covered with white stone, while the interior was covered with wall paintings that clearly imitated the style and composition of the nineteenth-century cathedral. Reality was quite different. This is visible, for example, in the materials used: concrete replaced brick, gold on the roofs was replaced by an alloy with a very low gold content, and bronze was used instead of marble for the exterior statues. To simplify this: the elegant and high-quality original was replaced by a "cheap" copy, a picture of many buildings (not only public) constructed in

Fig. 36: Conference room in the Cathedral of Christ the Saviour, 2019. Photo courtesy of the Ministry of Culture of the Republic of Crimea.

Russia in those years, where the rush to build was accompanied by the desire to maximize profits, thus producing monuments of poor quality.

However, the most radical changes were hidden under the floor of the cathedral: a garage with six hundred seats, a conference hall with one thousand seats, and a restaurant were built beneath the shell of the cathedral [Fig. 36]. These clearly commercial spaces provoked even more outraged reactions from many of the faithful: it was as if the whole cathedral was a kind of façade, while the commercial spaces represented the true content (or heart) of the monument. The cathedral was ready to open in September 1997, for the celebration of Moscow's 850th anniversary, but its underground space continued to cause great controversy. It represented an incredible combination of the new Russian Orthodoxy and the new economic system, which I think can be called without question "wild capitalism."[13]

---

13 Foletti, *The Cathedral of Christ the Savior*, 61–64.

Fig. 37: Church Holy Trinity, Moscow, 2004.
Photo courtsey of Andrey Korzun.

When I visited the cathedral in 2000, accompanied by my friends—intellectuals and ex-dissidents, but also Orthodox belonging to the persecuted church during the 1980s—there were only words of criticism. As Orthodox believers, they presented the building as an abuse of religion and the pre-revolutionary church in favour of the new lords. They also condemned the artistic and static design. In their view, it was so tragic that the building should have collapsed on its own in the next decade. Although this prophecy did not come true, it clearly shows us how the liberal (and Orthodox) intelligentsia viewed the whole project.

Despite all the criticisms, this reconstructed neo-neo-medieval building has become a symbol of a new chapter in the coexistence of church and state, just the way Yeltsin and Luzhkov wanted it. The desire to relate the state to the medieval and imperial past, at least in the form of a façade, has become one of the clear propaganda trends in Russia in the last decade. This was documented by the increasing number of churches built in the neo-Russian and neo-neo-Byzantine styles [Fig. 37]. This time, unlike in the years of Nicholas I, this neo-style was not backed by law as a national style, but, in reality, it was and is still used as if it were. Moreover, since at least 2000, a very shallowly formulated imperial rhetoric has been, and is, increasingly present in the public space, developed in parallel with the ever tighter coupling of the Orthodox Church and state.

Utilizing the original architectural model can be perceived as a form of going back in time: at least at the level of the façade, the imperial tradition of powerful Orthodox Russia is recalled. However, everything is fake in the new building: the Romanov's empire was inherently multicultural, while the new Orthodoxy of the 1990s was already taking shape in the context of the search for a new Russian identity with explicitly nationalist elements. Unlike in the Russia of the nineties, religion played an essential role in large sections of the population in the world before the revolution. Finally, the very idea of the "Middle Ages" was popular in the years of the last Romanovs, but absolutely alien to society after 1991, which was fascinated by modernity. The past—the nineteenth century and, through its filter, the Middle Ages—was used as a tool for the creation of a new Russian identity (and also, implicitly, as a tool for the exclusion of the "others"). This was, however, limited to the surface.

Furthermore, as already noted by the criticisms formulated at the moment of its erection, a deep schism was evident between the façade of the cathedral and its literal underground. On the one hand stood the official narrative of Russian Orthodox identity and, on the other, the interests of the new "wild capitalism" that had taken root in the country.

To some extent, the building could be compared to a Potemkin village: while the outer façade recalls the heroic past and its (apparent) virtues, the reality is quite different. The celebrated history of empire and Orthodoxy is merely a cover for the economic and political interests of elites who do not hesitate to use the past to manipulate the present.

A very similar situation—of "façade" work—can also be observed in the field of research. Byzantine studies and Russian medieval studies experienced a new "flowering" in the 1990s. The study of medieval Christian art was no longer heavily censored. In some cases, moreover, research returned to the ideological framework of the pre-revolutionary empire. After a seventy-year hiatus, it was possible to refer openly to early twentieth-century research, but also to the texts of white émigrés (i.e., those who left Russia after the October Revolution of 1917), which were strongly presented in an uncritical manner in many cases. Thus, some of the truly problematic imperialist theses of the early twentieth century returned to the public sphere.

Since colleagues active in the 1990s are still working, it is difficult to analyze this scholarly activity here in a proper historiographical way. However, it is evident that the situation in scholarship is similar to that which I have described above in relation to Christ the Saviour Cathedral. Byzantine studies experienced a *revival*, but its importance (like that of other humanities disciplines) was completely marginal to society. In the post-Soviet world with its free market dominated by figures of extremely wealthy oligarchs, often devoid of cultural background, historical studies no longer had anything to do with pre-revolutionary prestige (and funding), or even with Soviet social status. In 2005, I spent a higher amount of money on public transport to attend my first university lectures than the university was paying me per hour of teaching. Moreover, the impoverishment of the academic class led to a major crisis of knowledge. Excellent scholars of the Soviet period—who would finally have been able to publish freely—found themselves in the precarious position of accumulating different jobs that were often difficult to reconcile

with research. Ex-dissidents, who had not been able to publish in the past found themselves, after their initial enthusiasm, struggling for survival, often abandoning the field of
study. This led to the "freezing" of past knowledge in Russian
society to a large extent, a fact that made it particularly vul-
nerable to manipulation. The population remained basically
formed along the lines of a Soviet-style narrative, with only
a few surface changes. Such a situation was perfectly con-
venient for the new power, itself deeply rooted in the Soviet
past: since the 1990's repeated imperialist and religious slo-
gans and visual models that only faintly recalled the actual
imperial past for the purposes of contemporary propaganda
became sufficient tools. They completed the Soviet sub-layer
built on the myth of the invincible nation that had defeated
Napoleon and Hitler.

To finalize this landscape—albeit based on superficial
references to the past and a systematic weakening of critical research—of "revival" of the neo-medieval imperialist
tradition—one must remember the emergence of the cult of
the figure of the ruler and his moral "project" in contemporary Russia. Indeed, Vladimir Putin (and his entourage) was
trying to point out the parallel between his "rule" and that
of the Byzantine emperors, while affirming—as in the late
nineteenth century—the tradition of Moscow as the "Third
Rome."[14] The essential catalyzer in this process is undoubtedly the Moscow Patriarchate, which under the leadership of

---

14 It is a religious concept that originated in the fifteenth century. Moscow was supposed to save Christians on the run from
Constantinople, i.e.,the second Rome, which had fallen into the
hands of the Ottomans. By the end of the nineteenth century,
however, it had become an imperialist motive: the successor to
the Christian Roman Empire was to become Moscow. This issue
was discussed especially after Putin's visit to Mount Athos. The
president was wrongly accused of having sat on the Byzantine
imperial throne, which opened up an extensive debate in the
media. See, e.g., Anonymous, Игра в Престолы [Game of
Thrones].

the current Patriarch Kirill (since February 2009) has become the mouthpiece of the Kremlin, to some extent. The union of the church with Putin's regime has created a strange form of official discourse in which Orthodox "values" with a very conservative approach to various social issues are combined with state political interests. This certainly includes criticism of the decadent West and its "liberal values": patriarchy flanks the Kremlin in an increasingly homophobic policy and critique of "gender" issues. However, even in this case, one cannot shake off the impression that this is a "façade" yet again: statements of moral and ethical rigor are presented with pomp and circumstance, while the reality of Russian cities seems to have very little to do with these statements. And if, indeed, homosexuals are increasingly openly persecuted by the state apparatus, the real percentage of Orthodox believers is not only not increasing, but most of the population is increasingly indifferent to ideological issues.

To summarize what has been said, we can then consider that the reconstruction of the Cathedral of Christ the Saviour in Moscow can be seen as an emblematic operation in the creation of a façade masking underlying political greed, elitism, and corruption. In a country in the midst of economic crisis, struggling through dramatic convulsions caused by "shock therapy," and in search of its own new self, the cathedral was built to provide a purported new identity. In reality, however, this monument must be read above all as the ultimate expression that the new power had covered up—with a nineteenth-century façade—its true nature, which was and is that of a regime where the country's resources are exploited by a few very rich oligarchs, violent mobsters, and a state in the grip of corruption. In this sense, the Moscow cathedral can be seen as a particularly effective image of the whole relationship the country has—since the 1990s—with Orthodoxy and the (nineteenth-century and medieval) past it represents. Officially, religion and the past play a prominent role in Russian life, but the reality is very different—very few practicing Christians are actually there, while the "heroic past" has importance and room mainly in mass television culture.

Faced with this situation, one can then ask why Russian power has invested (and continues to invest) so much in what might seem like a "dead end track." I believe the answer comes from the fact that this "façade"—which since the nineteenth century, has easily allowed one to justify both a control of the local population and imperialistic pretensions—is terribly effective. In addition, Soviet and Russian education was built on a very sentimental pedagogical basis. This was particularly true for an almost religious experience of the monuments celebrating the past (being it the WWII or more distant events). Soviet and Russian citizens had to experience, within individual or shared performances of deep emotions, an idea of a fictitious brotherhood and possibly ignore in this way the dramas of the present. In this context, the heroic and imaginary Orthodox history became a very useful tool for post-Soviet Russian power. The official Orthodox Church, and in particular the Moscow Patriarchate, which has been considerably enriched over the years by this pragmatic union, has become one of the regime's most docile and effective accomplices for a large campaign of manipulation.

The Pussy Riot's Prayer: An Artistic Performance on a Neo-Medieval Backstage

A significant turning point in the context of an increasingly radical fusion of throne and altar, but also in terms of the use of a neo-medieval space, was represented by the so-called "punk prayer" performed by the group Pussy Riot in 2012 in the space of the Christ the Saviour Cathedral. During this performance, four women in balaclavas and colourful costumes danced and sang a prayer in which they begged the Mother of God to expel Patriarch Kirill and President Putin [Fig. 38]. The performance took place with their backs to the iconostasis, i.e., the barrier separating the space between clergy and laity, in the nave of the church, the space where women have the right to enter according to Orthodox custom. The prayer, which can be described as an engaged and performative work of art, presented the following lyrics:

Fig. 38: "Pussy Riot" in the Cathedral of Christ the Saviour, Moscow. Drawing by Janette Rendeková, 2024. Used with permission.

(Chorus)
Virgin Mary, Mother of God, banish Putin, banish Putin,
Virgin Mary, Mother of God, banish him, we pray thee!
Congregations genuflect,
Black robes brag gilt epaulettes,
Freedom's phantom's gone to heaven,
Gay Pride's chained and in detention.
KGB's chief saint descends
To guide the punks to prison vans.
Don't upset His Saintship, ladies,
Stick to making love and babies.
Crap, crap, this godliness crap!
Crap, crap, this holiness crap!
(Chorus)
Virgin Mary, Mother of God.
Be a feminist, we pray thee,
Be a feminist, we pray thee.
Bless our festering bastard-boss.
Let black cars parade the Cross.
The Missionary's in class for cash.

Meet him there, and pay his stash.
Patriarch Gundy believes in Putin.
Better believe in God, you vermin!
Fight for rights, forget the rite —
Join our protest, Holy Virgin.
(Chorus)
Virgin Mary, Mother of God, banish Putin, banish Putin,
Virgin Mary, Mother of God, we pray thee, banish him!

The words performed by the women artists are very explicit on three levels: first, they address the Virgin Mary with a supplication more or less in the canons of Christian tradition. Moreover, in the pure punk tradition, both the choreography and the words are clearly anti-conventional and in part vulgar (this is mainly visible in the double repetition, in the middle of the composition, of the sentence "Crap, crap, this godliness crap!"). The whole performance should be read as a radical critique of the political alliance between the state and the church.[15]

In most Russian media, however, this artistic and provocative event was presented as blasphemy against the Orthodox Church, and only consequently against Russia and Putin himself. The members of Pussy Riot were arrested and publicly tried for "hooliganism." The trial completely erased the political significance of the protest and made the whole event merely a blasphemous gesture against the Orthodox Church, from which the (believing) members of the group explicitly distanced themselves. Notwithstanding pressure from Western NGOs and political authorities, two members of Pussy Riot, Maria Alekhina and Nadezhda Tolokonnikova (at the time the mother of a two-year-old child), were sentenced to two years in prison.[16]

---

15 See e.g., J. Willems, *Pussy Riots Punk-Gebet: Religion, Recht und Politik in Russland* (Berlin: Berlin University Press, 2013); M. Gabowitsch, *Protest in Putin's Russia* (Cambridge: Polity, 2017), 160–94.

16 Anonymous, "Суд признал участниц Pussy Riot виновными в хулиганстве по мотивам религиозной ненависти и вражды

The performance held in the Cathedral of Christ the Saviour, which took the neo-neo-medieval context as a framework for an artistic engaged critique of the regime, had an important impact on both the perception of the Russian art scene in the 2010s and the shape of anti-Putin protests in the country. Finally, according to Mischa Gabowitsch, this event also paradoxically helped reinforce the link between the church and Putin's regime. For our purpose, one additional element is crucial: the neo-medieval building became the contested territory for defining Russia's role in the present world. Two national futures were put forth in the space that day. The first were those represented by a part of the Putin regime in union with the patriarchy, a regime that claims to base its identity on the past (and values) of the Orthodox empire of the last Romanovs. The alternative, provocatively embodied by Pussy Riot, was that of a liberal country integrated with tolerant and inclusive European cultural spaces.

To understand the reason for the claim to this sacred space, it is important to remember that the year 2012 was one of the turning points in the history of contemporary Russia. This was the year when Vladimir Putin returned to the leadership of the country after four years as prime minister, replacing Dimitry Medvedev. This was seen by many as a fraud on the electorate and an unprecedented wave of criticism arose within Russia. Millions of people, mainly liberal urban voters, took to the streets to protest [Fig. 39]. The Kremlin's heavy hand responded. Several opposition leaders and journalists died inexplicably, and opponents were arrested and convicted of fabricated crimes. Intimidation became an even more powerful tool of repression and caused a massive emigration of elites. Propaganda began to use all kinds of media, from TV channels to social networks to film productions, to present the Russian public with a worldview in harmony with the official doctrine of Putin's power.

[Court Finds Members of Pussy Riot Guilty of Rioting Based on Religious Hatred and Hostility].

Fig. 39: A column of protesters with the Cathedral of
Christ the Saviour in the background, Moscow, 2012.
Photo courtesy of A. Natotsinsky. Used with permission.

More important for this volume is that since 2012 an
increasingly aggressive rhetoric against the "Western" world
and its decadent values can be observed within Russian political and media spaces, with Pussy Riot's performance being
cited as the result of the decadent influence of the West. In
contrast, Orthodoxy rooted in the medieval (Russian and Byzantine) past, are portrayed in the public space as a positive
alternative and as inherently "Russian" values. On the basis
of a very simplistic interpretation of Russian philosophy and
theology, especially that of the nineteenth century, Russia
was presented as the only possible Christian alternative,
and as so different from the decadent West because it never
experienced a "Renaissance" and remained true to genuine
Christian qualities.

The performance by Pussy Riot enacted at the background
of Moscow's Christ the Saviour Cathedral seems instead to
be catalyzing, as perhaps hoped, protests against Vladimir
Putin's power, and it has become an essential moment in the
ideological framing of the current Russian regime. Held in
an iconic place for Russian reflection about itself and about

the past, this performance became the pretext for returning more than ever—in the rhetoric of official power—to Russia's "authentic tradition."

Neo-Medieval Propaganda: Preparing a War

The construction of an ideological system—no matter how superficial it may be—is certainly one of the interpretive lines for understanding the use of the medieval past to construct today's Russia. Furthermore, since the nineteenth century the medieval past has always been a powerful tool to justify even (and perhaps especially) the military expansion of the Russian Empire. It is not surprising that history has been actively used to explain the justness and legitimacy of today's military campaigns: as was clearly evident already during the 2008 annexation of the South Ossetian region in Georgia and even more so later during the first and second occupations of Ukrainian territory in 2014 and 2022.

Contemporary propaganda is particularly evident in the production of big-budget films and television series that increasingly highlight the heroic character of Orthodox Russian and Byzantine identity. Of interest in this sense is, for example, the highly successful TV show which started in 2016 about Sofia Palaiologina, a Russian princess of "Byzantine" origin. Russia's medieval roots, which are framed as stemming from the Byzantine Empire, are systematically emphasized in the show, and Saint Sofia of Kiev is presented as the cornerstone of Russian national identity.

The situation is obviously more complex: the current discourse on Kremlin power does not rely solely on the past as a mechanism to stage its present. Drawing even the barest contour of this situation brings us back to the beginning of this book and the construction of the Russian Armed Forces Cathedral. This building was conceived during a situation—at least in the joint rhetoric of the Kremlin, the patriarchate, and a part of the cultural sphere, in which "Holy Russia" was threatened on all sides both by military dangers and above all by the moral decadence of the West. In the idea of the builders of this church, the armed forces, together with Russian Orthodoxy, represented a bulwark of defence against all these evils. I have already written how much the architecture reminds one of iconic neo-medieval buildings of the nineteenth century. There are, however, other noteworthy elements, such as the underground baptistery, which is reminiscent of late antique models because of the shape of the font. This aspect is also emphasized by the aniconic decorations—which echo the models of the so-called mausoleum of Galla Placidia, a fifth-century Ravenna building—that are used on the vault above. The mosaic's figurative story also deserves recollection here: in broad strokes, the design is a revival of the narrative set of mosaics in the Moscow Metro. Broadly speaking, in fact, the heroic tale of the Russian people resisting Western evil follows the narrative structure of Komsomolskaya Station, a tale, as mentioned, inspired by Stalin's famous 1941 speech. We might say that the mosaics of the cathedral follow a "Stalinized" narrative.

This situation led to an overlap that is difficult to imagine and yet essential to the current Russian propaganda apparatus. These irreconcilable storylines straddle the heroic history of medieval Rus and the great victory in the Patriotic War waged by Stalin. Complementing this line of interpretation is a series of extremely evocative "details" found in and around the building. The so-called "memory walk" surrounding the religious complex is 1,418 steps long—the same number of days that the "Great patriotic war" against Hitler lasted. Some of the decorative elements were even cast using the first material weapons captured from the Nazi army in 1945 as mould models. Some of the major moments of the country's wartime glories—from the Alexander Nevsky victory to the taking of Berlin in 1945—were entered into a single linear narrative and framed, physically, by a neo-neo-medieval church intended to remind viewers of the reign of the last Romanov's. All the propagandistic tools of the Putin regime are found in a single setting. The war against great enemies of the past—from Teutonic knights to Nazi troops—must, therefore, be understood as a kind of unique holy war pitting

Orthodox Russia against the decadent West. The choice of major episodes for this narrative collage is not random, however: these were all moments when Russia was truly attacked by troops from the West. At first sight, the imperialist-Byzantine rhetoric and strong opposition to "Western values" are presented by Putin's entourage as a natural development of Russian identity, but also as a result of an "historical experience" in which the vile West did not hesitate to attack the country.

While the occupation by Napoleonic troops or that of Nazi troops certainly cannot be questioned (nor can the traumatizing effect of these events on Russia's collective identity be discounted), all available indications show that the current propaganda is primarily an ideological disguise. The strong neo-Roman and anti-Western rhetoric must be seen primarily as a reaction to the regime's internal problems. As already mentioned, in 2012 the regime had been severely challenged by millions of protests calling for the democratization of the country, but also for its modernization and the creation of a truly functional infrastructure. Its response has been a very aggressive attitude towards the internal opposition, imperialist and anti-Western rhetoric, and two successive wars again Ukraine. The propaganda of recent years, designed to create an external enemy, is, in my opinion, primarily the result of an "internal agenda." One is perhaps forced to admit that as a matter of the same "agenda," Putin's Russia has been working for the past decade on creating an external enemy. The past has been instrumental in justifying this attitude that has led—and not for the first time in the history of empires—to a first and then a second aggressive war. Today this same past is mobilized to explain why war is not only necessary, but holy, just, and unavoidable. It is not by chance the regime operates with the blessing of the Patriarch of All Russia.

In this regard, one last element must be mentioned. In June 2020, after the opening of the Armed Forces Cathedral, journalist Pavel Lobkov proposed a very critical analysis of the building. He regarded it, openly, as a warmongering project and criticized the flagrant union between patriarchy, patriarchate, and military power. One particular aspect struck me during his televized broadcast: he emphasized the fact that during the consecration ceremony, of those present—about two hundred selected, elite, guests—no one actively participated in the liturgy. He also emphasized that at the time of communion, five to six civilians and no military personnel approached the altar for the eucharist. Lobkov obviously wanted to point out a paradox: in this church for the military there is only an army of nonbelievers. This is perhaps the clearest proof of what is written above; Patriarch Kirill's Orthodoxy became a "public religion," a powerful tool of the state that is empty of believers. It allies itself with the throne to bless weapons and war, but it is itself a hollow shell, again a Potemkin village.

Conclusion

Contemporary Russia has created references through artistic outputs and in the media which are attached to the medieval past as part of a complex process rooted in a period of major transformations over the 1990s. A first line of interpretation is the official one that presents the "rebirth" of a neo-medieval and Orthodox tradition as the result of a return to the "real" roots of pre-revolutionary Russia. Since the years of the building of the Cathedral of Christ the Saviour in Moscow, however, an additional element has strongly emerged: it is the blatant manipulation of facts by the state and by Yeltsin and Putin in particular. Behind the façade of the Muscovite church lies a condensed vision of a Russia that has become, thanks to Yeltsin's "reforms," a country devoured by corruption and cronyism and, above all, a country that is governed by a lethal symbiosis between oligarchy and state thanks to these reforms.

Completing this diptych, however, is a third actor, the Moscow patriarchy, which provides present-day Russia with an ideological apparatus, conservative in nature, that is banal but paradoxically effective. Neo-medieval art, Byzantine studies, and also pop-culture help to spread this propaganda among the Russian population through official events and especially through various types of screens. What appears to an official glance as yet another return to Uvarov's triad—autocracy, orthodoxy, and nationality—is, in reality, a very different phenomenon: it is an absolutely superficial façade that has no real basis in either Russian history or culture. It fulfils its propagandistic purpose since it serves, with relative effectiveness, to justify its own expansionist and imperialist aspirations. Perhaps the most tragic aspect of this situation is the fact that all this has been done—and done quite effectively—to hide another reality. The Yeltsin and Putin administrations have turned this country into a desert, barren of identity, stripped of health, and hollow and hungry to believe in something, anything, to nourish and dissuade the collective trauma carried by all of Russia.

Conclusion

Trauma, Imperialism, and the Russia of Tomorrow

In the last two centuries or more, the Middle Ages, whether Russian or Byzantine, have become a powerful tool of propaganda and identity discourse for Russia. At crucial moments of crisis, medieval heritage has been used both visually and intellectually to affirm the country's imperial rights and to fight the external enemy. During the reign of the last Romanovs this situation seemed in some ways logical, and Russian rhetoric was essentially no different from that of other contemporary empires, but it was even more surprising (and complex) to uncover the (mis)use of the past in the Soviet years, when Stalin created a unique synthesis between the two seemingly contradictory trends of communism and clericalism. In the last two decades, then, it is possible to see a seeming return to the patterns that developed during the nineteenth century.

I hope I have been able to show that in each of the stages examined it is not so much the past itself that is interesting, but rather its use for the needs of the present. In this framework we can now return to the very beginning of this text, to Moscow's Cathedral of the Resurrection of Christ. All of the visual and material tools mentioned above and used therein tell a story of Russian identity. The building refers to the medieval past, but also to its reuse in the mid-twentieth century. This is evident not only in the architectural design but also in the iconography of the decoration. It is a celebration of medieval and modern warlords, with a strong reference to the decoration of the Stalinist underground, and to an idealized image of the national past. In light of the current situation, the 2020 construction can be seen as one of the crucial preparatory steps in the expansionist, imperial ambitions of the Russian Federation, which culminated in the military invasion of Ukraine in February 2022.

Visually and conceptually, the regime is following the rhetoric conveyed to the public by the mass media: that Moscow is the Third Rome, the last standard-bearer of Orthodoxy, and under its leader, it has a moral obligation to intervene, even with military force, against the evil that is rampant in the "fascist" West. It is clear, however, that something else is the goal of this huge propaganda effort. It is to make the Russian public forget the economic stagnation, the deep crisis of institutions, and the systemic injustices caused by the Putin regime. What could be a more effective means of manipulating the masses and uniting society behind a great leader than military conflict? At the same time, however, it is obvious that this propaganda is ultimately hollow. The Orthodox Church may be politically powerful, but Russia's churches are empty. The propaganda tradition of the nineteenth century, as well as its medieval heritage, have been transformed into shallow façades.

Going through more than two centuries of Russian history and imperialist developments in this country opens a further question: what are the deeper reasons for this aggressive and violent attitude? If we begin from the premise that, unfortunately, imperialism is one of the constants of human interaction, and not only over the past two centuries, the apparently cyclical nature of Russian history stands out nevertheless for its perpetuation of violent expansionism. A closer look reveals some interesting elements: first of all, one of the crucial features of this book has been the weight of the alleged "Byzantine" legacy. Over the centuries—from Enlightenment defamations to Orientalist scorn—"Byzantium" has become, in the common opinion, synonymous with a despotic, Eastern Empire. The "Byzantine" is—despite what we, scholars of the culture of the Eastern Roman Empire, think of it—perceived as archaic. Calling oneself its heir entails—willingly or unwillingly—taking an imperialist position.

The second element is certainly the covert aspect of neo-medieval ideology: from the reign of Nicholas I to that of Vladimir Putin, a thin thread that unites the economic and political interests of the empire is the secret police. Invented by Nicholas and brought to its zenith by Putin—a member of this institution—it is a body that always plots in the shadows. The neo-Byzantine or neo-Russian façade is a perfect cover to conceal the true (imperialistic) intentions of those who run the country.

One last element must unfortunately be evoked, however: Russian imperialist excesses were, throughout the nineteenth and twentieth centuries, stimulated by both domestic propaganda and by aggressions by Western countries. I refer both to the Napoleonic wars and the Nazi invasion but also in part to the Crimean War in 1855—although in this case the situation was more complex. Imperialist expansion in those years seems intimately linked to a play of "action and reaction" that constitutes Russian identity. One further aspect also needs to be remembered: the invasion of Napoleonic troops and especially that of the Nazi army corresponded to moments of absolute chaos and drama that heavily (and rightly, I might add) traumatized the Russian mindset. This is in no way a justification of Russian imperialism of the past centuries, but rather a reflection to how the "action-reaction" mechanism works in geopolitics. Moreover, the greater the collective trauma, the greater the danger of a reaction. Russian imperialism during the nineteenth century and that of the USSR after World War II have their roots precisely in these shared traumas, which are so easy to exploit by propaganda. Trauma begets fear, and fear is easy to manipulate.

What is the reason for the imperialist madness we are witnessing in Russia today? The answer I have tried to give in the last chapter of this book goes back to the country's collapse in the early 1990s. With nearly half the population sunk below the poverty line and with a staggering mortality rate—some speak of 10 percent of the population disappear-

Fig. 40: Opposition rally ahead of presidential elections. The text on the poster references a legendary song by Russian rocker Victor Tsoi "I want changes," which, at one point, became a hymn of Perestroika. Photo courtesy of D. Kyndrová. Used with permission.

ing (and emigrating) in the first five years after 1991—the collective trauma is close to that of a war. And it is on this potential of fear that Putin's regime is built. As we all know, history cannot be rewritten and yet I cannot free myself from questioning what the world would be like today if, instead of being abandoned to collapse, Russia had been supported like Germany (and Europe) by some form of a Marshall Plan.

* * *

The last time I was in Moscow—just a few months before the start of the coronavirus pandemic—the city was already very different from how I remembered it twenty years ago. It was clean, orderly, but the city centre lacked the incredible energy that characterized it after the fall of the USSR.

My friends were at home as always, working, taking care of disabled people, fighting for human rights, working for MEMORIAL. But there was a tiredness in their voices, a sadness in their faces. They talked openly about the "Soviet Renaissance" and their desire to emigrate. Some did so before February 24, 2022, others immediately afterwards. A few staunch activists resolutely stayed behind to care for the disabled people who could not leave the country. What is evident, however, is that Putin's regime has literally let the country bleed to death by driving the vast majority of its intellectual elites out. Even those whose families did not flee the Bolsheviks have left the country. To manipulate the population that remains, the Putin regime is content with the pathetic and superficial imperialist arsenal that is the subject of this book, and with the constant rehashing of the time-honoured story of victory over Hitler. However, I ask myself: when will all this finally come to an end? When will there finally be a change in Russia that will not cause another catastrophe like the 1990s? When will Russia finally be part of the family of democratic states as Václav Havel (1936–2011) wished in his legendary speech to the U.S. Congress? The dissident Havel, who had been freed only a few months earlier from communist imprisonment and had meanwhile been elected president of the republic, delivered an incredible speech to the U.S. Congress, February 21, 1990:

> I often hear the question of how the United States can help us today. My answer is paradoxical, as it has been all my life: you can help us most by helping the Soviet Union on its irreversible but still extremely complicated path to democracy. It is a far more complicated path than its former European satellites can follow. ...It is therefore not for me to advise you. All I can say is that the sooner, the faster, and the more peacefully the Soviet Union starts to follow the path of real political pluralism, respect for the rights of peoples to self-government and a functioning, i.e. market economy, the better it will be not only for the Czechs and Slovaks, but for the whole world.

These few words sum up the political greatness of the man Havel, a person capable of seeing beyond hatreds and fears. Imprisoned and humiliated for years by the communist regime, a prime witness to the Soviet (and other Warsaw Pact countries') invasion of Czechoslovakia in August 1968, Havel believed in a future based on reconciliation. He also knew from a very pragmatic perspective, however, that nothing is more dangerous than an "exploded" Russia—the events of 1917 and, unfortunately today, those of the early 1990s proved this to him and to many others. If only Congress had had the wisdom to listen to him.

I do not know when that will happen, but it is clear that, just as Havel predicted, Russia will need, and does need, our help. I sincerely hope that this time the "West" will be wiser and will not let the country collapse again. Until then, like the girl in Dana Kyndrova's beautiful photograph, I will wait for change [Fig. 40].

Further Reading

Historical Documents

Examples of Western newspaper coverage of recent topical events

Sachs, Jeffrey D. "Russia's Tumultuous Decade: An Insider Remembers." *The Washington Monthly*, March 2000. https://web.archive.org/web/20000407085843/http://www.washingtonmonthly.com/books/2000/0003.sachs.html, accessed March 19, 2023.

Sandford, Daniel. "Russian Election: Biggest Protests since Fall of USSR." *BBC News*, December 10, 2011. https://www.bbc.com/news/world-europe-16122524, accessed March 17, 2023.

Examples of Russian coverage of recent topical events

Anonymous. "Игра в Престолы: Почему России больше 500 лет остается в тренде византийской политики? [Game of Thrones: Why Has Russia Remained in the Trend of Byzantine Politics for More than 500 Years?]." *Газета.ru* 30, no. 5 (2016). https://www.gazeta.ru/comments/2016/05/30_e_8271917.shtml, accessed March 3, 2023.

——. "Суд признал участниц Pussy Riot виновными в хулиганстве по мотивам религиозной ненависти и вражды [Court Finds Members of Pussy Riot Guilty of Rioting Based on Religious Hatred and Hostility]." *TASS*, August 17, 2012. https://tass.ru/arhiv/587327, accessed March 17, 2023.

Arkadiev, Andrey. "Главный храм Вооруженных сил РФ получил статус Патриаршего собора РПЦ [The Main Cathedral of the Armed Forces of the Russian Federation Has Been Granted the Status of the Patriarchal Cathedral of the Russian Orthodox Church]." *Телеканал Звезда* [TV Channel Star], February 6, 2020. https://tvzvezda.ru/news/2020261536-sD2Jb.html, accessed March 17, 2023.

Selected Russian nineteenth-century sources relevant for the topic

Gagarin, Grigory. *Краткая хронологическая таблица в пособие истории византийского искусства* [A Short Chronological Table in the Handbook on the History of Byzantine Art]. Tbilisi: Tipografiya Kancelariya Namestnika Kavkazskogo, 1856.

"Манифест к грузинскому народу, 12(24). сентября 1801 года [Manifesto to the Georgian Nation, 12 (24). September 1801]." In *Полное собрание законов Российской Империи с 1649 года* [Complete Collection of the Laws of the Russian Empire since 1649]. Saint Petersburg: Otdeleniya Sobstvennoj Ego Imperatorskogo Velichestva kancelyarii, 1830.

"Статья 218 Устава Строительного [Article 218 of the Statutes of the Construction]."

Sultanov, Nikolai. "Русское зодчество в западной оценке: Критический разбор [Russian Architecture in Western Evaluation: Critical Analysis]." *Зодчий* [Architect] 1 (1880): 6–12.

In *Свод законов Российской Империи: Уставы путей сообщения, почтовый, телеграфический, строительный, и пожарный* [Code of Laws of the Russian Empire: Statutes of Communication Routes, Postal, Telegraphic, Construction, and Fire Charters], 12. Saint Petersburg: Otdeleniya Sobstvennoj Ego Imperatorskogo Velichestva kancelyarii, 1857.

Thon, Konstantin. *Проекты церквей, сочиненные архитектором его имп: Величества профессором архитектуры Императорской Академии художеств и члена разных иностранных академий Константином Тоном* [Church Designs Devised by the Imperial Architect: Professor of Architecture at the Imperial Academy of Painting and Member of Various Foreign Academies Konstantin Thon]. Saint Petersburg, 1844.

Chapter 1 Texts

Histories on neo-medieval Russian architecture

Butikov, Georgy. *The Church of the Saviour on the Blood*. Saint Petersburg: Museum of Church of Saviour on the Blood, 1996.

Wortman, Richard. "The 'Russian Style' in Church Architecture as Imperial Symbol after 1881." In *Architectures of Russian Identity: 1500 to the Present*. Edited by James Cracraft and Daniel B. Rowland, 101–229. Ithaca: Cornell University Press, 2003.

Scholarship devoted to the history of Russian studies

Foletti, Ivan. *From Byzantium to Holy Russia: Nikodim Kondakov (1844–1925) and the Invention of the Icon*. Rome: Viella, 2017.

——, and Pavel Rakitin. "From Russia with Love: The First Russian Studies on the Art of the Southern Caucasus." *Venezia Arti* 27 (December 2018): 15–35.

Lidova, Maria. "The Rise of Byzantine Art and Archaeology in Late Imperial Russia." In *Empires of Faith in Late Antiquity*. Edited by Jaś Elsner, 120–60. Cambridge: Cambridge University Press, 2020.

Russian political identity during the last decades of the Romanov Empire

Aizlewood, Robin. "Revisiting Russian Identity in Russian Thought: From Chaadaev to the Early Twentieth Century." *The Slavonic and East European Review* 78, no. 1 (January 2000): 20–43.

Lieven, Dominic. *Russia Against Napoleon: The Battle for Europe, 1807 to 1814*. London: Penguin, 2009.

Rakitin, Pavel. "Byzantine Echoes in the Nineteenth-Century Press and in the Writings of Russian Intellectuals." In *Byzantium, Russia and Europe: Meeting and Construction of Worlds*. Edited by Ivan Foletti and Zuzana Frantová, 98–109. Brno: Masaryk University, 2013.

Wortman, Richard. *Scenarios of Power: Myth and Ceremony in Russian Monarchy from Peter the Great to the Abdication of Nicholas II*. Princeton: Princeton University Press, 2006.

Chapter 2 Texts

Soviet architecture during the first half of the twentieth century

Kazus', Igor'. *Sovetskaya architektura 1920-ch godov: Organizacija proektirovanija* [Soviet Architecture in the 1920s: Organization of Design]. Moscow, 2009.

Paperny, Vladimir. *Architecture in the Age of Stalin: Culture Two*. Cambridge: Cambridge University Press, 2002.

Taroutina, Maria. *The Icon and the Square: Russian Modernism and the Russo-Byzantine Revival*. Pennsylvania: Penn State University Press, 2018.

Udovicki-Selb, Danilo. "Between Modernism and Socialist Realism: Soviet Architectural Culture under Stalin's Revolution from Above, 1928-1938." *Journal of the Society of Architectural Historians* 68, no. 4 (2009): 467-95.

Scholarship devoted to the history of Russian studies

Foletti, Ivan and Adrien Palladino. *Byzantium or Democracy? Kondakov's Legacy in Emigration: The Institutum Kondakovianum and André Grabar, 1925-1952*. Rome: Viella, 2020.

Political and national context of the USSR

Berthon, Simon and Johana Potts. *Warlords: An Extraordinary Recreation of World War II Through the Eyes and Minds of Hitler, Churchill, Roosevelt, and Stalin*. Boston: Da Capo, 2007.

Dehaan, Heather D. *Stalinist City Planning: Professionals, Performance, and Power*. Toronto: University of Toronto Press, 2013.

Hewryk, Titus D. *The Lost Architecture of Kiev*. New York: Ukrainian Museum, 1982.

Merritt Miner, Steven. *Stalin's Holy War: Religion, Nationalism, and Alliance Politics, 1941-1945*. Chapel Hill: University of North Carolina Press, 2003.

Navrotskaya, Anna. "Aleksandr Nevskii: Hagiography and National Biography." *Cahiers du monde russe* 46, no. 1-2 (2005): 297-304.

Snyder, Timothy. *Bloodlands: Europe Between Hitler and Stalin.* New York: Basic, 2010.

Chapter 3 Texts

Late-twentieth and early twenty-first century Russian architecture

Smith, Kathleen. "An Old Cathedral for a New Russia: The Symbolic Politics of the Reconstituted Church of Christ the Saviour." *Religion, State and Society* 25, no. 2 (1997): 163-75.

Late-twentieth and early twenty-first century Russian political and national context

Beissinger, Mark R. "Nationalism and the Collapse of Soviet Communism." *Contemporary European History* 18, no. 3 (2008): 331-47.

Duncan, Peter J. S. "Contemporary Russian Identity between East and West." *The Historical Journal* 48, no. 1 (2005): 277-93.

Edwards, Allyson and Roberto Rabbia. "The 'Wild Nineties': Youth Engagement, Memory and Continuities between Yeltsin's and Putin's Russia." In *Youth and Memory in Europe: Defining the Past, Shaping the Future.* Edited by Félix Friess, Nina Friess, 75-83. Berlin: De Gruyter 2022.

Gabowitsch, Mischa. *Protest in Putin's Russia.* Cambridge: Polity, 2017.

Kotz, David M. and Fred Weir. *Russia's Path from Gorbachev to Putin: The Demise of the Soviet System and the New Russia.* London: Routledge, 2007.

Russian social and economic history in the 1990s

Miller, Chris. *The Struggle to Save the Soviet Economy: Mikhail Gorbachev and the Collapse of the USSR.* Chapel Hill: University of North Carolina Press, 2016.

Silverman, Bertram and Murray Yanowitch. *New Rich, New Poor, New Russia Winners and Losers on the Russian Road to Capitalism.* New York: Routledge, 2000.

Printed in the United States
by Baker & Taylor Publisher Services